Penetration Testing

Penetration Testing

Robert Shimonski

A Wiley Brand

Penetration Testing For Dummies®

Published by: **John Wiley & Sons, Inc.,** 111 River Street, Hoboken, NJ 07030-5774, www.wiley.com

Copyright © 2020 by John Wiley & Sons, Inc., Hoboken, New Jersey

Published simultaneously in Canada

For general information on our other products and services, please contact our Customer Care Department within the U.S. at 877-762-2974, outside the U.S. at 317-572-3993, or fax 317-572-4002. For technical support, please visit https://hub.wiley.com/community/support/dummies.

Wiley publishes in a variety of print and electronic formats and by print-on-demand. Some material included with standard print versions of this book may not be included in e-books or in print-on-demand. If this book refers to media such as a CD or DVD that is not included in the version you purchased, you may download this material at http://booksupport.wiley.com. For more information about Wiley products, visit www.wiley.com.

Library of Congress Control Number: 2020934346

ISBN 978-1-119-57748-5 (pbk); ISBN 978-1-119-57747-8 (ebk); ISBN 978-1-119-57746-1 (ebk)

Contents at a Glance

Table of Contents

Introduction

Welcome to *Penetration Testing For Dummies*! It is my goal to start you down the path to learning more about pen testing and why it's such a hot topic for anyone interested in information technology security. This book shows you how to target, test, analyze, and report on security vulnerabilities with pen testing tools.

I break down the most complex of topics into easily digestible chunks that familiarize you with the details of conducting a pen test, but also why you need to do it and how the hackers you are trying to access your systems are doing so. Your purpose as a pen tester is to test systems, identify risks, and then mitigate those risks before the hackers do.

It takes a person with hacking skills to look for the weaknesses that make an organization susceptible to hacking. The topics in this book aim to equip IT professionals at various levels with the basic knowledge of pen testing.

About This Book

One of my main goals in writing this book is to give you an understanding of the different attacks, vectors, vulnerabilities, patterns, and paths that hackers use to get into your network and systems. Pen testing is intended to follow those same steps, so security pros know about them (and can fix or monitor them) before the hackers do.

For this book, I use a Windows workstation and where I must, I use Linux tools run from a virtual machine. I have chosen this because this is where many beginners are likely to start their pen testing journey. For this book, you can use any current supported version of Windows (Windows 7 and above) on a device that has a network connection (wired and wireless).

A highly experienced pen tester will likely use a native Linux system like Ubuntu (as an example), but you do not need to use it now.

If you are using Linux or Apple, you can follow the same steps throughout the book with a few modifications here and there.

Foolish Assumptions

As I was writing this book, I assumed you work in IT and want to transition to security. It is the go-to book for those who have some IT experience but desire more knowledge of how to gather intelligence on a target, learn the steps for mapping out a test, and discover best practices for analyzing, solving, and reporting on vulnerabilities.

You might have an entry-level or junior position, or you might be a manager or director, with more experience but coming from a different area of expertise. Either way, you want to know more about how pen testing fits into the big picture. As such, you'll find that I explain even simple concepts to clarify things in the context of penetration testing and overall security.

Icons Used in This Book

Throughout the book, I use various icons to draw your attention to specific information. Here's a list of those icons and what they mean.

TIP

This icon highlights pointers where I provide an easier way of doing something or info that can save you time. This icon points to content you definitely don't want to miss, so be sure to read whatever's next to it.

REMEMBER

When you see this icon, you know it's next to information to keep in mind — or something I've discussed elsewhere, and I'm reminding you of it. It's often advice to help keep you out of trouble.

WARNING

Pay close attention to this icon, which I use to point out pitfalls to avoid or where doing something (or not doing something) could land you in legal trouble (like pen testing something you don't have permission to test).

TECHNICAL STUFF

Sometimes I provide particularly sticky details about an issue, which can get technical and which may not be of interest (or help). You could ignore any text marked with this icon, and you won't miss it a whit.

What You're Not to Read

This book is written so you aren't required to read it beginning to end. If you're familiar with the basics of penetration testing, for example, you can probably skip the first part. You can skip Part 2 if you feel you have a pretty good handle on attack types and various pen testing tools. Technical Stuff icons are truly technical pieces of information that I file under "nice to know" — skip those, as well, if you're looking for need-to-know content only.

Where to Go from Here

If you're truly new to the world of penetration testing, I recommend you begin with Chapter 1 and read from there. Readers with a grasp on pen testing fundamentals — what it is, the role of the pen tester, types of hackers, types of attacks, and so on — but who want to hone their testing and/or reporting skills, for example, can go straight to Parts 3 and 4, respectively.

Looking for information about a particular tool or attack? Use the Table of Contents or Index to find where I cover that thing and go straight to that discussion. More advanced readers might want to read only those sections that cover any area they need to bone up on.

Of course, I recommend Chapters 15 and 16 for everyone because continual learning is so important to becoming and remaining an excellent pen tester.

You can also find more pen testing topics on the book's cheat sheet, such as pen testing terminology and specific certifications you'll find useful in your career. Go to dummies.com and search for "Pen Testing For Dummies cheat sheet" to find it.

REMEMBER

The more you study, read, and work in the field, the more you'll learn as your journey continues. It can be something you eventually have a really good understanding of . . . but by that time, the technology will have changed many times! As a journey of lifelong learning and study that can be very rewarding and exciting as you progress, becoming a pen tester is a true commitment.

1

Getting Started with Pen Testing

IN THIS CHAPTER

» **Exploring pen testing positions**

» **Discovering what tests and certs you need for pen testing**

» **Understanding what skills are necessary for pen testing**

» **Considering cybercrime**

» **Doing your first pen test**

Chapter **1**

Understanding the Role Pen Testers Play in Security

Penetration (or pen, for short) testing is one of the hottest up and coming skills any IT professional needs to have. As more and more technology takes over our world, the need to ensure it's safe and secure is at the forefront. Companies are actively looking for professionals with a background in IT security and the ability to do penetration testing.

As a pen tester, you need a solid understanding of how an attacker can access your systems and how they can conduct attacks. Not to fear, I walk you through these attacks and the mind of the hacker. You have to truly think like a hacker to be a good pen tester, which is why pen testers are called white hats, grey hats, or ethical hackers, which I explain in more depth in Chapter 2.

I also lay out everything you need to know about security vulnerabilities and introduce you to the tools, techniques, and skills that today's most elite pen testers use on a daily basis to conduct penetration tests that keep their company's assets safe.

I get to all that and more throughout the book, but in this chapter, I cover the basics, starting with what roles a pen tester can hold in a company. I move from there into the importance of getting certified and what skills are required. I end the chapter with a couple sections that can set you on the path to becoming a competent and sought-after pen tester.

Looking at Pen Testing Roles

The security arena has myriad names applied to anyone who does good or bad security stuff. If you're new to pen testing, all that can be highly confusing. To clear up any and all confusion on the matter, I dedicate this section to describing the good guys who do pen testing and what roles you might have as a pen tester. (See Chapter 2 for a breakdown of the baddies.)

The pen tester's role is to penetrate and to ethically hack to find weaknesses within a company's IT security program. Securing the weaknesses might be someone else's responsibility. You may or may not be responsible for making recommendations based on the weaknesses you uncover, but I discuss that task in Chapter 12.

WARNING

You must have permission to conduct penetration testing if you don't work in the field or for a company hired to conduct it. Even if you're hired to pen test an organization's security, you likely still need permission for certain types of pen testing activities. See Chapter 9 for more on that issue.

Crowdsourced pen testers

As big data grows as a concept and more and more systems grow in complexity and size, especially as companies move into cloud architecture and outsourced solutions, there is a need to leverage additional resources to stay on top of all the latest risks, issues, and threats. As more and more systems join massive compute models and virtualized systems are used in new architectural models, the global community of good guys (white hat hackers) can bring a wide array of benefits to the table.

Crowdsourcing is a form of security where pen testing is done via group-based team efforts of enthusiasts (who can also be experts) for the purpose of testing systems managed by enterprises much the same way a constant group may. For example, a crowdsource pen test group may be contacted to run the same types of attacks against you that a consultant may and report on their findings.

Crowdsourced pen testing is no different than any other crowdsourced solution. You're using multiple resources to conduct your tasks to get a better outcome by leveraging a large pool of resources, knowledge, and abilities. But if you're concerned about privacy and legal exposure, go with a consultant.

You can find crowdsourcers at sites such as www.hackerone.com. Join and offer your services or find pen testers to help you out with a project.

In-house security pro

In-house security operations versus consulting services for hire (which I discuss in the next section) are generally how pen testers work in the field. Large companies and government agencies generally employ in-house operations engineers who conduct pen tests for the business they work for.

Smaller organizations can't always afford to keep staff of this kind, and they often don't have enough work to keep them busy. Sometimes conducting pen tests isn't a dedicated position but is a task given to a systems administrator, a network engineer, or other IT professional in the organization.

An in-house employee who's dedicated to securing the organization's interests, assets, and reputation is often called a security analyst. This is someone employed full-time by a company, firm, or business (public, private, non-profit, government, military, or otherwise) who is responsible for providing security services. That's a broad term for what can be a very detailed role requiring a variety of security functions, the skills needed, and the tools that are used.

Depending on the organization and the exact role, security analysts might have many other names, such as these (not a complete list):

>> Chief Information Security Officer (CISO)

>> Security architect

>> Security engineer

>> Security operations staff

>> Risk analyst

>> Forensics technician

>> Security practitioner

These are obviously more detailed roles within security, but they all work with security, and they all analyze security at some level of degree.

Generally, to become a good security analyst you need to absorb, learn, or train in many other areas so you have a holistic view of the enterprise you are charged with securing. I discuss what you need to know in the later section, "Gaining the Basic Skills to Pen Test."

Security consultant

You can hire a consultant to conduct a pen test for you or your firm. Consultants are for hire either as independent contractors or as part of firms you can hire. This may save you time and money in the future.

Consultants at times work for firms that specialize in security or provide security services under a contract. This means that they can scan remotely (externally) or come onsite and scan internally and do more intrusive testing. Either way, consultants allow a smaller organization to retain top talent for a reasonable price and still get the services needed to be current and secure. This route also paves the way for those entering into the field of pen testing an opportunity to gain employment through a company or a contract to conduct security services.

Getting Certified

Professional organizations and vendors both offer industry standard, generalized and specialized certification programs, as well as those based on specific vendor tools. Some of them mix the two.

For example, one of the biggest and most focused pen testing certifications on the market today is CompTIA's pentest+ certification. Although it covers general topics on pen testing, it also goes in depth on the tools you use the most. There are also other certifications, such as the CEH (certified ethical hacker certification) and the SANS GIAC Penetration Testing certification (covered in Chapter 16).

You can also start with general security certifications such as the CompTIA Security+ or the ISC2 CISSP.

TIP

It would also benefit you to learn how to write and submit reports and present your findings. I cover these topics in detail in Part 4.

Gaining the Basic Skills to Pen Test

You're going to need a wide variety of skills throughout your pen testing career, but the biggest (or most important) skills to have are in the realm of networking and general security, which I discuss in this section.

TAKING A HOLISTIC VIEW OF SECURITY

Having an understanding of an organization's business model and industry will enable you to take a holistic approach to security practices. Gaining that holistic view may require programming, network engineering, and system engineering, as well as understanding endpoints, desktops, storage, and many other systems and services. This doesn't mean you can't practice security if you don't have all these other skills, but it definitely makes a difference on your ability to strategize and lead a security effort, and/or be able to respond to security threats, breaches, and attacks with better efficiency.

Security in a holistic view is also known as *defense in depth*. Confidentiality, integrity, and availability (CIA) make up a triad and defense in depth and pen testing helps to secure it, which is essentially the entire holistic view of practicing security in an organization.

To be able to conduct a pen test with any amount of confidence, the more you know about security and network architecture, the better. For example, to run a basic pen test, you need to enter a network address or subnet range in your scanning tool.

You need to also know the difference between vulnerability scanning and pen testing and why they're similar and how they're different. Figure 1-1 shows the basics of setting up an IP addressing range to scan and identify vulnerabilities. After you know the risks and weaknesses, you can then move into the details on how to exploit (pen test) what has been found so you can learn whether the technology is secured.

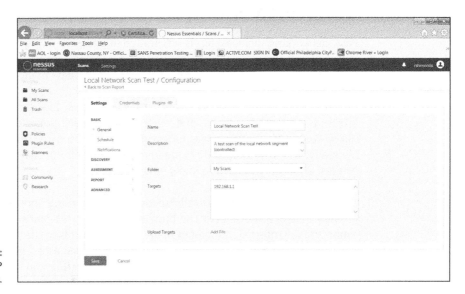

FIGURE 1-1: Adding an IP range to scan.

It's also crucial to understand IP, protocols, networking, and other technologies related (and also not directly related) to security analysis because as weaknesses are identified (perhaps with a scan), then you can then move to exploit them (pen test) no matter what technology you're presented with (database, mainframes, virtualized systems, for example).

In the following sections, I outline what knowledge you need to be a successful pen tester.

REMEMBER

No stone is unturned as a pen tester, and what you need to expect is everything and anything. You are tested just as much as the systems you're testing. Additionally, criminal activity isn't confined to computers. The Internet of things (IOT) is an ever-expanding network of connected devices that includes, but is not limited to, tablets, phones, and smarthome devices such as TVs and thermostats. You may not encounter all those devices working as a professional pen tester in the corporate world, but you need to be aware of all connected devices. And when you're pen testing, take time to find out which devices could be affected, such as mobile devices and assets used by field staff.

TIP

Also be aware of a hacker's reconnaissance procedures. Hackers often begin attacks by using general research techniques, such as Internet searches that point a hacker in a direction, to learn more about accessing your company. For example, a simple Whois search might provide an address. A DNS search or query could provide a clue. Google searches may help to identify paths of attack, URLs, domain names, IPs, email addresses, and more. See Chapter 2 for more about reconnaissance.

Basic networking

Basic networking includes, but is not limited to, understanding the OSI (open systems interconnect) model. Knowing how data transits from one location (a sender) to another (a receiver) is key to being able to unwind how many attacks occur.

It also includes knowing how routers, switches, hubs, load balancers, firewalls, intrusion prevention devices, and other network black boxes on the wire work. (*Black-box security testing* refers to testing software security from the outside in. Generally, the tester has little or no knowledge of the internal workings.) If you pen test a router, you need to know how it operates.

The TCP/IP protocol suite also falls under basic networking knowledge. The transmission control protocol (TCP) and Internet protocol (IP) controls how computers connect to the Internet. It includes many of the protocols in the 7-layer OSI model. The Open Systems Interconnection (OSI) model is used as a logical framework to show how data travels from the source to the destination and back to the source through the many technologies that comprise the network, systems, and applications. It's a model of standards that shows the under the hood actions of the technologies at each layer. Figure 1-2 shows an example of the OSI model.

Application
Presentation
Session
Transport
Network
Data Link
Physical

FIGURE 1-2: Examining the OSI model.

The protocols used in a suite (such as TCP/IP) map to the various layers of the model and perform different functions. For example, FTP operates at a higher layer in the model than TCP or IP. The theory is that, if the lower layers don't work, then the higher layer protocols won't operate correctly. The OSI allows you to troubleshoot problems in a workflow manner.

Figure 1-3 shows a wire packet capture that shows a lot of the information you need to read through to conduct a pen test with a tool such as Wireshark. Here you can see packets that when captured can be decoded to tell you the details within them.

Having knowledge of these protocols, how and where they operate, and what is contained in the frames, headers, and other inner details of the packet is what will make you a great pen tester. If you run a pen test and it reports back, for example, that you have a vulnerability in telnet that's sending packets back and forth in cleartext, you need to determine what path a hacker may take. You can more easily make that determination if you know how the protocols work and what is expected behavior and what can be manipulated versus what could be impacted by a software bug. This way, you can test it yourself first to identify whether you have an issue that might need to be remediated or mitigated.

TIP

I highly recommend that you study more on TCP/IP. It's the main protocol suite in use today across the world; when it was first put into production many years ago it came with many flaws. Its ease of use is one of the biggest flaws and the fact that security was an afterthought behind usability. That said, today's networks and systems can account for these flaws, but there is always danger in the shadows. Study TCP/IP and all of its sub-protocols and how they work to get better at testing weaknesses in your enterprise.

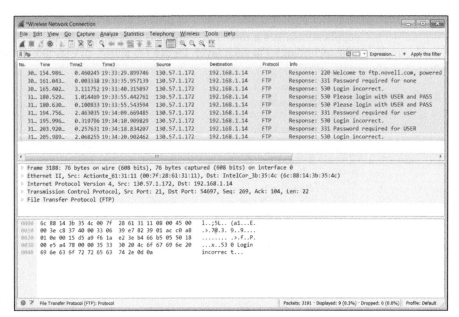

FIGURE 1-3:
Digging into a
network packet
capture.

General security technology

In the general security technology category are firewalls. Most scans against devices such as a firewall turn up little to no information. Knowing why is helpful to your report. For example, in a ping sweep, you ping the interface and find nothing because the firewall has disabled that protocol that responds.

Figure 1-4 shows a Cisco router firewall log that lists the source and destination IP addresses used to make each connection as well as a description of what that connection did.

Another example is when you run a scan and find open ports are in use on a web server in a DMZ behind a firewall that shouldn't be. By examining the firewall log that sits in front of these servers, you can see what the source IP address is that's attempting to make those connections. You can detail it as an active attack and prioritize it immediately to patch or fix.

Other general yet important technologies to consider would be devices such as intrusion prevention and detection systems, load balancers, access control lists (ACLs) on routers and wireless access points, controllers, and mobile extenders. Each and every one of these devices all can be exploited and the more you know about them and how to review the logs on them, the better you are at identifying risks and conducting ethical hacking.

Severity	Syslog ID	Source IP	Source Port	Destination IP	Destination Port
i 6	725003	10.0.220.13	59043		
i 6	725001	10.0.220.13	59043		
i 6	302013	10.0.220.13	59043	10.0.0.1	4433
i 6	302020	10.0.220.13	11	10.2.2.36	0
i 6	302013	10.0.220.13	59041	50.19.236.61	80
i 6	305011	10.0.220.13	59041	12.178.152.131	59041
i 6	302013	10.0.220.13	59040	50.19.236.61	80
i 6	305011	10.0.220.13	59040	12.178.152.131	59040
i 6	106015	10.0.220.13	57973	10.0.0.1	4433
i 6	106015	10.0.220.13	57968	10.0.0.1	4433
i 6	106015	10.0.220.13	57967	10.0.0.1	4433
i 6	106015	10.0.220.13	57969	10.0.0.1	4433
i 6	106015	10.0.220.13	57971	10.0.0.1	4433
i 6	106015	10.0.220.13	57974	10.0.0.1	4433
i 6	106015	10.0.220.13	57972	10.0.0.1	4433
i 6	106015	10.0.220.13	57970	10.0.0.1	4433
i 6	106015	10.0.220.13	59038	10.0.0.1	4433

FIGURE 1-4: Review a firewall log.

Systems infrastructure and applications

You must also be familiar with a company's systems (servers, storage, and tele-communications) and the applications that run on them. This includes operating systems and the services they offer (name resolution services, remote access gateways, and IP address leasing). Pen testing any and all these areas will show up on your reports.

If you run a scan on a Domain Name System (DNS) you may find that it needs to be patched. If the server is a Microsoft Windows Server system, you may be able to download needed patches and apply them based on the report. You may also be running a UNIX or Linux system running BIND, which is a DNS name daemon or service. Either way, both may show up on your report as needing attention. Know-ing what they are can help you to direct attention towards not only how to repair them, but also which must be prioritized immediately.

Web applications and web programming are also major areas that are exposed to vulnerabilities based on the logic needed to keep them running. Database servers running the Structured Query Language (SQL) may be subject to injection attacks. Operating systems that the services and applications run on also remain open to attack and need to be scanned and patched.

Mobile and cloud

Mobile technology is also a must-know endpoint technology quickly replacing the desktops and other devices. They also travel to and from locations and absolutely must be addressed — whether the devices are company assets or company software and data used on a personal device. There are challenges with this system, which mobile device management (MDM) solutions help overcome.

You might worry about testing them to make sure they're secure, but you approach this like you approach all the other systems you're accountable for — you scan, test, and report based on your findings and handle the risks as you identify them.

Cloud is another boundary IT security pros are trying to cross in the world of security and pen testing. Because cloud technologies fall under the purview of their cloud provider, as long as you're working in conjunction with the cloud provider's security team and they're conducing pen tests, then you have achieved the same goal as if you did it yourself.

Note: You might face the fallout of mistakes or mishaps committed on the vendor side.

Introducing Cybercrime

Cybercrime is the act of conducting criminal activities — for example, data theft, information destruction, and identify theft — using technology such as computer systems and networks. A lot of hacking revolves around cyber activities and cybercrime. Any access to something that is done *not* with the intention of doing an investigation, including collecting information about access or damage (harm), is in fact against the law. As time has passed, more and more legal aspects of protecting assets has arisen since the earlier 1990s.

Here are some key considerations about cybercrime you should consider before you pen test:

>> Those who commit cybercrime are usually out to gain information, access, or leverage to create a competitive edge, or gain wealth or information that can be used or sold.

>> The main way that cybercriminals conduct these criminal activities is by surreptitiously accessing information systems to get resources.

>> The only way to know how vulnerable you are to cybercrime activities is to test your systems yourself. This enables you to be ahead of the curve in protecting these resources and assets to mitigate risk.

>> You must be employed, contracted, or given permission to conduct ethical hacking, pen testing, vulnerability testing, or any other assessment where computer technology will be penetrated and exploited to find vulnerabilities.

WARNING

Pen testing can be considered an act of cyberwarfare if you test on systems and networks you don't have permission to test on. It reverts your ethical hacking procedures into unethical ones with that simple oversight!

If you don't work in the field and/or for a company hired to conduct pen testing, you must have permission to conduct it.

REMEMBER

>> Once vulnerabilities are found, you can use the tools to exploit them. However, you must be careful to analyze what that could impact or other problems it could create. For example, you can overwhelm a buffer on a network card or network switch to test its ability to be exploited, creating an outage in the network or on the system.

>> You should be careful and assess whether possible irreversible damage can be caused and plan for it. What this means is you might conduct an exploit that could corrupt an operating system and if that happens, it must be restored to get it back to working condition.

>> You must be careful not to corrupt (or lose) data as part of the host system, storage unit, server, or other storage facility. Make sure a full backup is done prior to testing.

>> You could expose weaknesses to others you might be working with and that could cause problems with information being leaked about security issues that then impact a company's reputation. This is why it's recommended to be very careful with giving any information to anyone who doesn't need to know.

>> If you're the security incident handler (like those on an Incident Response Team, which I discuss in Chapter 2) who's tracking a cybercriminal, you might be responsible for collecting data and creating a chain of custody of the evidence that can be used in a court of law.

>> The dark web (or darknet) is where many attackers go to find their tools as this part of the web is normally not searchable with common search engines. Most of these tools are found on peer to peer networks and other means of distribution and are the leading causes of attacks via script kiddies and low level hackers worldwide. Most cybercrime (and cyberwarfare) is conducted using these means.

WARNING

CROSSING THE LINE INTO CYBERTERRORISM AND CYBERWARFARE

Cybercrime is also known as *cyberterrorism* and *cyberwarfare* and can be considered an act of war, especially with foreign actors. Say, for example, someone in Russia runs a few tools acquired on the dark web to penetrate U.S. businesses — to gain access, for instance. One could consider that an act of war or terrorism.

It can get even worse if those same countries (or others) decide to launch attacks to disable power grids, steal secrets, or gain access to military secrets. This makes pen testing and ensuring assets are secure very important. Just as important is re-testing to ensure they remain secure over time.

What You Need to Get Started

You might not realize it, but you don't just dive into pen testing. You should take these specific steps before you get into the heart of pen testing:

>> **Make sure you have a thorough understanding of the basics of information technology (IT) systems, networks, and other technologies at the fundamental level.** This knowledge aids your career in security, pen testing, and ethical hacking.

>> **Conduct vulnerability tests.** A type of pen testing is a vulnerability test. A vulnerability test identifies in advance any potential threats — areas where a hacker could potentially attack a vector — to your systems. An *attack vector* is a method or pathway a hacker uses to access or penetrate the target system; hackers poke around your systems to find something that's weak or vulnerable. I discuss vectors in further detail in Chapter 4. One example of a vulnerability is a known software bug that allows elevated privileges.

You'll use framework tools such as Metasploit (see Figure 1-5) and other tools to produce vulnerability reports that detail all the security concerns you need to know. From there, you can run additional tests to determine exactly what you need to do (if anything) to fix the threat.

TIP

Vulnerability tests become more complex and exponentially more useful when you use them in combination with other tests. Other tests may include, but aren't limited to, system checks (for example, checking logs for access), vulnerability logs, and system performance tests that show items such as high CPU, disk utilization, or other system issues that could potentially show an exposure, breach, or injection of code or an unwanted visitor.

>> **Consider when to scan.** It might seem obvious, but when you decide to scan is also important. To keep vectors as secure as possible, you need to set up schedules in which you scan, during specific and regular intervals, that cover all areas of the enterprise in which you aim to protect.

>> **Choose which tools to use.** Figure 1-5 shows Metasploit (which I discuss further in Chapter 4), a tool you can use to run scans. There are many management and monitoring tools, logs, and other software to augment your pen test to have a complete view of the holes in your security. I cover many of these tools in Chapter 3 and discuss additional tools and sources throughout Part 2.

>> **Test in a safe environment.** You'll want to test all changes and new scans in a lab (*sandbox*) prior to unleashing them on your production systems, to make sure you know what they will do before you cause more impact.

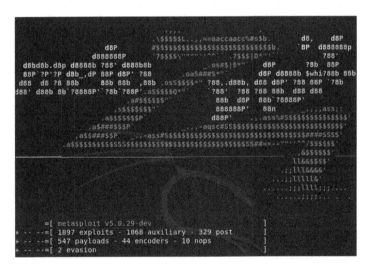

FIGURE 1-5:
Metasploit is one tool for pen testing.

Deciding How and When to Pen Test

When you conduct any pen test, your goal is to have a strategy.

You can blindly run tests to see what you find; you can also try to penetrate systems to find whether there are any weaknesses. That's fine for any scans or tests you conduct weekly or monthly to assess your overall *security posture*, which is the status of the security of your company's software and hardware, networks, services, and information. The state of your security posture should be evaluated regularly and take into account your readiness and ability to react to and recover from incidents.

Sometimes you want to go deeper and really test your security posture by conducting specific attacks, such as penetration, stealth operations, destroy attacks, and overwhelm attacks. For example, if you believe a hacker's goal is to gain access to files from outside of your corporate network, your goal should be to assess that threat using your tools.

You also want to conduct both internal and external tests. You never know where your attacks might originate from.

TIP

A high-level view of what vectors an attack may come from— both those from within your trusted network (with trusted users) and those that originate from outside of your security perimeter from untrusted users — is essential to have. An example of an external attack from an outside untrusted user may come in the form of someone using a website you host in your network (usually in a demilitarized zone [DMZ]) that may find a vulnerability that allows them to access resources from within your trusted network. On the contrary, an internal attack is just that — originating from inside your network that easily evades all the perimeter security such as firewalls and access control lists.

Either way, you can run scans using Nessus (see Figure 1-6) to see whether either of those vectors produce the result you don't want, which is a hacker gaining access to your systems without your knowledge.

I discuss how to select the right tool and analyze for weaknesses that could cause your enterprise, brand, and data great harm if not fixed or monitored in Part 2.

FIGURE 1-6:
Use Nessus to
conduct an
assessment.

REMEMBER

You need to find the right balance between security and assessment. You might know of a hack, but not be able to fix it. A completely 100 percent secure system is usually unusable to anyone. Networks and systems were made to be used and that means leaving ports open. For example, the Internet generally requires that port 80 (HTTP) be left open.

Taking Your First Steps

When you're ready to pen test, these are the general steps you'll take:

1. **Download and run a pen test tool in a safe environment such as your home.**

WARNING

Running a pen test in a production environment that causes an outage is a denial of service attack, which prevents other people from using your system. Make sure you're doing things safely and as controlled as possible to test and find risks, not create outages and impact. I discuss denial of service attacks more in Chapter 6.

2. **Download a free tool and start to investigate.**

I discuss many available tools in Chapter 3, but for a basic test, I recommend using a vulnerability scanner. Figure 1-7 shows Retina CS from BeyondTrust (www.beyondtrust.com), which allows you to run scans to see what a host is susceptible to and what threats are exposed.

3. **Scan a single host by its IP address, or an entire IP subnet with many hosts on it.**

This step helps you identify target systems that need to be reviewed based on the reports they generate for threats and exploits that may exist on them.

4. **Document the host or hosts you're testing and then which attacks you want to try based on the information you have gathered.**

Your goal here is to find vulnerabilities.

5. **Penetrate.**

This is the part of the pen test that actually conducts the known hack to see if you can execute it.

6. **Follow up with your findings.**

You can report the findings, fix the issues, monitor the issues that don't have fixes, contact the vendors to get fixes, block access, and so on.

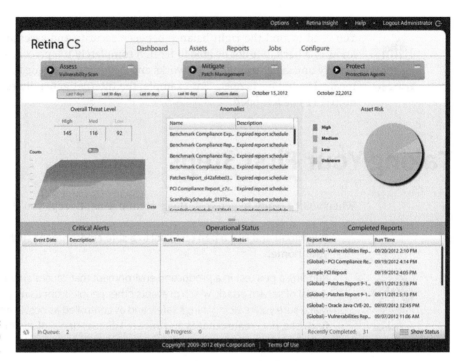

FIGURE 1-7:
Examining a
Retina CS scan.

Chapter **2**

An Overview Look at Pen Testing

P en testers are the cops of the network. They make sure people aren't break-ing rules and getting themselves or others into trouble. Hackers — be they white, grey, or black — are always out there actively trying to thwart secu-rity systems and access systems that they shouldn't be accessing.

In this chapter, I give you the knowledge you need to become the cop of your net-work: the goals of good pen testers, the importance of ongoing scanning, and how tell the good hackers from the bad.

The Goals of Pen Testing

The ultimate goal to penetration testing is to test your technology assets for their security, their safeguards, and controls by trying to penetrate through any config-ured defenses. But pen testing can be broken down into individual smaller goals.

REMEMBER

Pen testing, although a hot topic, isn't a new concept nor is it an incredibly diffi-cult one. The underlying technologies, concepts, and techniques can go very deep. However, conducting pen testing can be very easy if you're trained and have the right knowledge. (See Chapter 1 where I discuss which skills are necessary for pen testing.) The breadth of pen testing is where the complexity grows because net-works, systems, infrastructure, mobility, and cloud architecture all stretch what needs to be assessed. That requires you to look at every aspect of everything your client, company, or business is accountable for.

Protecting assets

Your goal as a security analyst (one of the good guys) should be to keep the bad guys (hackers) out of things that they should not be in. It's important to protect assets so that they can't be damaged or corrupted (rendering them unusable), altered (changed), infected (with a virus), stolen, hijacked, or the myriad of other security threats that could happen.

This list breaks down various security scenarios by industry type:

» **The banking industry:** Money can be stolen, moved to other accounts, or debt added to others.

» **Credit card industry:** Identities are stolen and that information is used to penetrate accounts that have monetary assets or credit that can be used.

» **The sales industry:** Patents can be stolen and products made outside in foreign competitor companies, which causes businesses to fail and stock prices to drop (or rise) based on the intention of the hacker.

» **Health industry:** Electronic medical record (EMR) systems can be infiltrated to change, gather, or corrupt info.

» **Power industry:** The power grid needs to stay online, so the government, private industry, and residents can access energy to carry on daily tasks.

» **Military (and other governmental) industries:** Secrets need to stay secret and information can't be obtained to cause harm.

REMEMBER

You can be proactive by conducting daily, weekly, monthly, quarterly, and yearly tests to find weaknesses that can be monitored or fixed.

Identifying risk

Risk is another important word to define prior to discussing vulnerabilities. What is at risk is the technology that runs much of our world today and the data that resides on that technology. By testing that technology, pen testers can reduce the risk of it being exploited and causing harm. What is at risk is simple. . . security itself is at risk.

Risks run the gamut regarding what level of damage might be done if the risk isn't mitigated properly although you don't necessarily handle all risks the same:

>> **A small, identified risk:** The risk can be small where you know there is a problem, but you accept its risk because you can't fix it at this time. Maybe a patch is not yet available by a software vendor and you need to wait.

>> **An identified risk to monitor:** You identify a risk and monitor it, but a penetration and exploitation would lead to very little threat. An example may be hurting the company's reputation slightly by upsetting a few clients who rely on the systems because they temporarily weren't available. This risk is low level.

There are also other situations where some vulnerabilities can't be exploited, and it makes sense to monitor them. Other vulnerabilities can be exploited and are of a very high priority (and risk) and therefore must be monitored until they're corrected, which may take some time to accomplish.

>> **An identified high-risk ripe to be exploited:** This risk is likely to be exploited and may cause loss to a company's finances, high-level reputation, or worse, a loss of life.

You record all these risks in a risk register and log the results of most security assessments (your pen test results) with a marker denoting the level of risk and the priority in which it should be addressed.

A *risk register* is a list of known risks and vulnerabilities that you compile as you scan, assess, penetrate, and test. The risk register is the official document (or information stored and accessible in a database, spreadsheet, or other facility) that shows the following:

>> What risks (and vulnerabilities) you've found

>> How you may have found those risks

>> The weight you've assigned to each risk

>> A priority level in fixing or correcting each risk

REMEMBER

Sometimes you have to simply accept a few vulnerabilities in the course of getting business done. Systems are upgraded, new sites are added, mergers and joint ventures happen. But it's still important for you to know where they are, so you can keep an eye on unusual activity through that vulnerability.

Table 2-1 shows what a typical risk register looks like.

TABLE 2-1

A Risk Register

Risk Register Entry #	Risk Category	Risk Sub-category
1	Security	Virus
2	Network	Wireless
3	Power	UPS
4	Environmental	Fire Suppression
5	Datacenter	Space
6	Environmental	Fire Suppression
7	Environmental	HVAC
8	Security	Physical
9	Server	Operating System
10	Datacenter	Consolidation
11	Storage	Capacity
12	Storage	Capacity
13	Security	HIPPA And PHI
14	Database	Backup
15	Database	Corruption
16	Database	Network
17	Datacenter	Space

The risk register is a great tool to help you identify problems, but it would be hard to guess what changes could cause problems, which is why companies have pen testing conducted: to test their systems for weaknesses. A company might have an in-house team doing the testing or outsource to a security firm or individual consultant.

REMEMBER

Testing continues throughout the year(s) — perhaps weekly, monthly or quarterly — to ensure you find all the problems that may have surfaced or been exposed.

A risk register is a living document that you're constantly updating. I talk more about it in Chapter 11.

Finding vulnerabilities

A *vulnerability* is simply a weakness that can be exploited in your technology or something as simple as information disclosure. The technology weakness can be through misconfiguration of an asset, a bug, or code problem in the software installed, or any anomaly in your enterprise.

For example, your hardware vendor updated your firewall, inadvertently introducing a bug. You can be completely unaware of the exploit until either it's identified by the vendor or another end user, or you run a pen test on your firewall. This doesn't mean all bugs are exploits, but some can cause and lead to exploits.

Vulnerabilities are a type of risk that can be rated and used as a recorded artifact that can be logged, reviewed, and corrected by people who are responsible for its correction.

Two examples of vulnerabilities are:

>> **A buffer overflow:** *Buffers* are memory spaces in computers, systems, routers, switches, and many devices in your infrastructure that help to speed up things and make transferring data more efficient. For example, two devices communicating may get impacted by one sending way too much data for the other one to absorb and compute, so it may buffer it (send it into memory, essentially slowing it down) for a moment to let the internal computing of the receiving system catch up.

   Malware (malicious software) is a type of exploit created by a hacker that can take this seemingly good service and turn it into a vulnerability. If a malicious party now sends too much data to the buffer in an effort to exploit a weakness and overwhelm (or overflow) it, it could cause performance to be impacted or in the worst-case scenario, crash the system or cause it to be unresponsive.

>> **Password usage:** Weak passwords (easily guessed or easily cracked with a password cracking tool) allow immediate entry into a system with the click of the tools button. This is a real-world example of a very common vulnerability, which can be found and prevented by a pen test.

   A good corporate password policy (with a system that secures and enforces it) is the best chance to protect against this vulnerability. Unfortunately, it's still common in many places around the world, and I'm sure during your own pen testing, you will find instances of it during your own pen testing.

Chapter 6 covers other vulnerabilities.

Scanning and assessing

The successful pen tester uses tools (both hardware and software) to run penetration tests (sometimes also called *penetration assessments*) to find vulnerabilities and exploit them.

You scan for vulnerabilities on your system, network, or entire enterprise to find risks that you can either fix or acknowledge. Figure 2-1 shows a scan from Nessus (scanning software), which I cover (along with other tools) more in depth in Chapter 3.

FIGURE 2-1:
Sample output
from Nessus.

WARNING

Never run a pen test, assessment, scan, or security test on a live production network without permission! Many things can go wrong. For example, you could run a scan on a segment of the network configured with devices to block penetration attempts that shut services off that could impact a production system that's servicing clients. Another example: In a hospital system, if you decide to run a scan during the day on a protected network segment without making some adjustments, it could shut down services and prevent patients from receiving care.

Securing operations

Typical security operations conducted in an enterprise range from simple to complex. It all depends on many factors, including size of the company, importance of the assets, available budget, leadership's interest in any (or all) of these factors, and the knowledge and skills of those entrusted to secure and keep secure the assets of the enterprise. To do this, you can either conduct your own security assessments, outsource them, and in some cases even crowdsource them.

DEFENSE IN DEPTH

Defense in depth is a concept that requires you to consider all the ways an asset can be exploited and add layers of security to it — in this way, you create some defensive depth. A great example of adding a layer of security is dual-factor authentication. If I log into a system using a password, having to provide a second password (or better, a biometric control or a code that's emailed or texted to me) adds another layer of proving who I am — in a way that others cannot easily replicate — to access the asset.

Pen testing can help to validate whether systems have defense in depth. If, for example, a simple password cracking test easily smashes open a defense, you know that you can make the recommendation that the company needs to use harder to guess passwords via a good policy. If the password-protected asset is of high value, you could recommend using a secondary method (such as dual-factor authentication) of authorization to protect it.

Responding to incidents

What if you can see an active attack taking place because of issues you identified through pen testing and which you are now monitoring as part of your ongoing risk assessment? The answer lies in a process or workflow called *incident response.*

Incident response (which is sometimes called *incident handling*) is the event management of an attack based on an exploitation of a known or unknown vulnerability. In this book, I'm primarily focused on conducting pen tests and how to prevent attacks, so I don't spend much time explaining incident response or incident handling. As a security analyst, however, you should know what an incident response team (IRT) is and why it exists. That's what I briefly explain in this section.

You might wonder why you'd need a specialized team to handle security-related issues, and the answer is actually very simple: The need is based on containing the incident. Special training is required, and special procedures must be followed for an incident to be handled correctly, as these examples show:

>> **A need-to-know basis:** You don't want to tip off someone conducting an active attack that you know it's happening and are watching. To prevent the attacker from knowing their movements are being monitored, who needs to know about the attack as it happens will be restricted to trained individuals who can react appropriately to the incident.

>> **Containing the chain of custody on evidence:** You might also want to control the actual message of the day as the incident could wind up on social media platforms or the evening news. You just never know how an incident may impact you or your organization, so you have specific handling procedures and a trained team in place to handle the details.

Note that one part of containing the event is to provide tangible evidence in a court of law. Should the company decide to take legal action against the perpetrator, documented evidence will be needed.

What do you do if you have an active incident take place? The answer depends on the following:

>> **Where you are:** Location is everything! If you're local to the attack you can start to work the issue and can conduct all tests and other actions without fear of being disconnected from the network. If you're working on a virtual private network (VPN) connection or remotely connected to a system over a network, it may be part of the attack vector and you could become disconnected. Being local to the system allows you console access directly from the system itself and in most cases, this can be the most reliable option.

>> **Who you are (that is, what role you have):** To be designated an active member of an IRT, you simply need to be assigned the role. It may be a full-time role in a larger organization or consulting firms, or in smaller firms you may be assigned it as a collateral duty. Either way, the responsibility is the same and understanding your role and the procedures, processes, and plans are important.

The actual team you're assigned to needs to train together. There is value in understanding everyone's place on the team and how to handle an active incident.

>> **What you believe to be happening:** Most companies have an IRT that's responsible for providing support in the case of an active incident handling request, such as a firewall breach, a virus or malware outbreak, an intrusion, or any other security-related matter. What event is actually happening dictates your course of action.

Obviously, you don't ever want to have to respond to an active attack. Hopefully, you might be able to prevent it in the first place, and that is why pen testing is so valuable in the entire security framework and defense in depth. If you're able to secure everything properly or identify any weaknesses and fix them (or accept and monitor them), you solve half the exploit battle.

Scanning Maintenance

I want to shift focus now to what pen testing and constantly scanning for exploits looks like in a real-world scenario or in a corporate security plan. The truth is that what pen testing actually looks like depends on the organization and the value and budget it puts into the actual security team's ability to test, assess, and fix.

Regardless, you can't just scan all day long and scan whenever you want. Most times, you need to gain approvals to run scans. But you need to know what those scans are and what they're scanning for. I discuss a few in this section.

Exclusions and ping sweeps

You need to test systems, and you might have to create *exclusions*, which are systems you can't scan. Knowing which systems you can't scan is very important. For example, you may have very old and antiquated systems; scanning them may cause an outage to the system. You may have older systems that run critical functions that you're aware need to be replaced or upgraded, but the software vendor may not have released patches or current software for your older hardware. Maybe they won't ever release updates because they no longer support these platforms. Whatever the case, you may have to exclude these systems from your scan and test them in a different way.

Additionally, you may have to tune certain scans on specific systems so that they don't trip defenses on that system. A great example of that is a firewall. Firewalls don't like *ping sweeps* (which is the repeat testing with ICMP using the ping tool to see what systems respond). There may be access control lists (ACLs) in place or firewall rules that block these requests. You may not be able to reach certain segments because the routing won't allow for a return path and you won't be able to get the results of your scan. These are just a few reasons why you must understand scan maintenance moving forward if you want to implement a professional pen testing program in your organization.

REMEMBER

One of the most commonly used TCP/IP suite protocols is Internet Control Message Protocol (ICMP). ICMP messages are used to conduct ping sweeps in most scanning tools. The scan can be used to test hosts on the network for ports that are open or hosts that are responsive. If I can query a host and know it accepts my communication — and I also find a door to knock on (an open port) — then my job as a hacker is as easy as conducting a brute force attack on the host to find a way in.

Open ports indicate services that may be running and listening on a device that may be susceptible to an attack. Open ports can provide an entry point. Ping sweeps use ICMP to touch the hosts on the network and a tool such as Nmap (shown in Figure 2-2 and which I cover in more detail in Chapter 8) can be used to attempt IP and port combinations to find what the ping is answering to.

```
root@legacy:~
File   Edit   View   Terminal   Help
[root@legacy ~]# nmap -sP 172.24.0.*

Starting Nmap 5.21 ( http://nmap.org ) at 2010-08-29 10:12 IST
Nmap scan report for 172.24.0.1
Host is up (0.0015s latency).
MAC Address: 00:21:29:89:76:B6 (Cisco-Linksys)
Nmap scan report for 172.24.0.11
Host is up (0.00014s latency).
MAC Address: 00:1D:92:DD:83:7C (Micro-star Int'l Co.)
Nmap scan report for 172.24.0.33
Host is up (0.00013s latency).
MAC Address: 00:1D:92:42:9D:A9 (Micro-star Int'l Co.)
Nmap scan report for 172.24.0.119
Host is up (0.00014s latency).
MAC Address: 00:1D:92:3F:DE:14 (Micro-star Int'l Co.)
Nmap scan report for 172.24.0.128
Host is up (0.00011s latency).
MAC Address: 00:24:8C:C6:16:A7 (Asustek Computer)
Nmap scan report for 172.24.0.142
Host is up (0.00016s latency).
MAC Address: 00:1D:92:42:9D:57 (Micro-star Int'l Co.)
Nmap scan report for 172.24.0.147
Host is up (0.00021s latency).
MAC Address: B8:AC:6F:5E:1E:EC (Unknown)
Nmap scan report for 172.24.0.149
Host is up (0.00013s latency).
MAC Address: 00:24:8C:C6:2F:44 (Asustek Computer)
Nmap scan report for 172.24.0.250
Host is up (0.000092s latency).
MAC Address: 00:E0:4D:9E:61:0C (Internet Initiative Japan)
Nmap scan report for legacy (172.24.0.252)
Host is up.
Nmap done: 256 IP addresses (10 hosts up) scanned in 2.42 seconds
[root@legacy ~]#
```

FIGURE 2-2:
Nmap is a tool you use to conduct to ping sweeps.

Port scanners scan only for open ports. A vulnerability scanner can do much more than that, and it can then conduct other probes to find out-of-date software, mis-configurations, and more. This is where a tool such as Nessus (which I introduce in Chapter 3) becomes more valuable to the pen tester.

Patching

System patching is one of the main outcomes of at least half the items on your risk register. Because software is often so buggy (even upon release — see the nearby sidebar), over half of the results and solutions provided by your software vendors and almost all of your "bugs" found in code results in an exploit. Service packs, hotfixes, firmware updates, upgrades, and hardening by patching can solve many of your problems.

WARNING

Aside from buggy code, the second biggest reason why mishaps such as exploited vulnerabilities and attacks take place is because something isn't configured correctly or configured correctly and then altered so that a vulnerability is inadvertently exposed on the system.

MOST SOFTWARE VENDORS RELEASE BUGGY CODE

It's a scary truth, but it's a truth all the same: Most software vendors do in fact release buggy code. What this means is that there's no way a software vendor — whether they make a simple network card driver, an application, or an operating system — can fix every single problem before they release the product to the public. This is why most software vendors have beta programs, beta testing, early release programs, and test software deployments. They will use that time to identify issues with the code and will actively identify and patch with software revisions.

Code developers spend a large amount of time running these tests and attempt to release the best software possible. With today's demands and requirements for more, more, more, however, it's just not feasible to release a perfect product without a bug or two.

For example, you might have a bulletproof Linux server but by adding a web server such as Apache to it, you might have opened some ports or exposed something that puts the server at risk.

Again, if you do some pen testing and scan the server (and the web server), you can find those open ports or access points and then identify, secure, and/or configure them so that there are no further issues to worry about.

Antivirus and other technologies

When considering how pen testing works, it's helpful to understand the basics of heuristical scanning, which is very much like vulnerability assessment. An AV program sits on a system and is fed information to run a baseline and look for anomalies. If anything comes up and is a match for a known piece of malware, for example, or just looks weird in general, the AV quarantines it for inspection. Figure 2-3 highlights commonly used AV software.

Other similar technologies such as intrusion detection software (IDS) and intrusion prevention software (IPS) actively scan traffic for exploits, malware, intrusion attempts, and other anomalies. They work similarly to how AV programs and pen test tools such as Nessus do. Although I don't cover AV/IDS and IPS in this book because they're not traditional toolsets used by pen testers, the truth is that you will need to use them to understand the scope of any attacks.

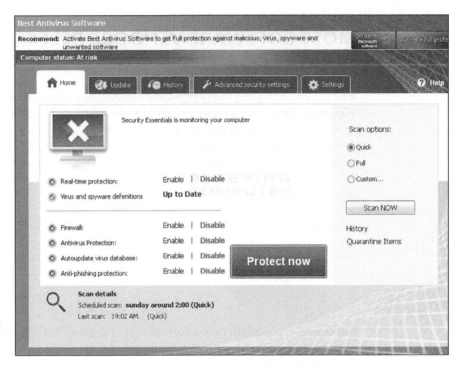

FIGURE 2-3:
Examples of
commonly used
AV programs.

Another consideration is, what if you hardened everything and used all of the security architecture possible to secure your systems? If you designed and implemented your systems and networks correctly, understood and tested for every change before making any, and only installed and used stable, well-tested, and non-problematic code, you would really never have any security-related issues. If you added a secure perimeter defense system with firewalls, IPS/IDS units, and active monitoring, you would be worry free!

The fact is, this is just not reality. You make changes. You connect to other companies and vendors to do business. You install code that isn't ready for prime time. You do work and function in these infrastructures and dynamically build them as you go, so you can anticipate that there will be some issues. Because of that you would absolutely need to pen test!

Compliance

Another consideration in your pen testing activities is whether your company needs to meet a compliance level. I cover compliance, reporting, and legal matters in an upcoming chapter, but I bring this up now because pen testing isn't only to secure systems and networks. Your company might be legally obligated to ensure (and prove) they're doing everything possible to protect information that anyone entrusts to their organization. This means you must have a way to determine and prove that compliance is met.

Here are just two (although common) standards of compliance:

» **Payment Card Industry Data Security Standard (PCI DSS):** This is a compliance standard that organizations must uphold to use credit cards, hold cardholder data, and safeguard against fraud. Pen testing and risk compliance are big components toward the compliance of this standard.

» **Health Insurance Portability and Accountability Act (HIPAA) of 1996:** This was put into effect as a piece of United States legislation to ensure that patient privacy is guaranteed by health providers, who are held to high standards, audited, and fined heavily if not compliant.

Other industries have other standards of compliance. Always be sure you're aware of any compliance issues and what it takes to maintain compliance.

Hacker Agenda

An integral piece of this chapter is to talk about who you're fighting: the bad guys, otherwise known as *hackers*. The problem with calling them hackers is that, technically, the good guys are hackers, too. The whole culture is confusing, so I attempt to demystify it with simple explanations of a myriad of definitions.

First, forget the good and bad of it. Think neutral — a hacker is someone who likes to pull apart computers, systems, code, or applications to further investigate, test, probe, or learn from them because they're intrigued. That's it! That's how simple it really is. Your typical hacker is someone who likes to noodle with technology.

Now, I consider motives. I cover bad guys, so you can better understand your enemy. In some situations, however, the bad guys might become your allies. Some elite hackers have joined forces with law enforcement as part of their plea bargains and have shown them their skills!

I also cover the most commonly used terms in the hacker community today to denote and identify who's a good guy (white hat), a bad guy (black hat), or somewhere in the middle (grey hat).

Hackivist

A *hacktivist* (someone who promotes hacktivism) wants to use technology in a way to promote their agendas, which are generally centered around a political movement or social effort. One of the best examples of modern hacktivism is the group Anonymous. Although they're not the first (some, like the Cult of the Dead Cow, have been around for many, many years), they have proven to be one of the most widely seen on social media platforms and even in pop culture.

The motive is to use technology assets to get something they want. So, if a hacktivist wants to enact a change in a political agenda, they may penetrate a series of web servers and deface them in hopes to embarrass or motivate others in a particular way against their political adversary.

With pen testing, you would have been able to scan those web servers, find that they could be exploited and protected. Unfortunately, hacktivists run their own secure scanners to find the weakness to exploit them.

Script kiddie to elite

There are two ends of the spectrum, and you need to understand the type and volume of both sides.

Elite hackers in the world intimately understand not only the systems and structures but also how to program them, make tools that can penetrate systems, and exploit them. These elite hackers are few and far between but are highly dangerous. They only get caught when they make a big mistake that exposes them because most times they spoof where they originate from and are very hard to identify.

On the other side of the spectrum are *script kiddies.* Script kiddies have basic skills and just enough knowledge to be dangerous. They download and gain access to the tools the elite hackers create and follow their blueprints to gain access to systems and cause problems. Although they're nowhere near as skilled or dangerous as the elite hackers, they can become a threat if they're able to pull off an attack successfully.

White hat

White hat hackers are you and I: Those who practice security are security analysts and do pen testing to protect technology assets. White hats are those who can legitimately duplicate hacks but to test for vulnerabilities and exploits and secure them. White hats are responsible for conducting hack attacks in secure labs to study the outcomes so they're understood and what risks they impose.

Grey hat

Grey hat hackers are those who border on the white and the black. They may not be as malicious as a black hat hacker, but they cross the lines at times and break laws, steal corporate code, or even share information they shouldn't. The grey hat is usually someone who doesn't work as a security analyst or in another security role in an organization but isn't a criminal looking to break laws and risk imprisonment.

Black hat

Black hat hackers are hackers who want to exploit systems and technology for personal gain. They either want to seek revenge, get a financial payment, or gain another benefit from conducting attacks on systems. If a black hat hacker finds something they can exploit, they do so without question — especially if it fits their motives. They also go on social channels (such as the dark web) and share this information openly, sometimes creating a multi-prong attack against others (or entities) in the form of distributed attacks, such as a distributed denial of service (DDoS) attack. Black hat hackers are indeed criminals and are generally found or caught and penalized (and sometimes imprisoned) for their actions.

Doing Active Reconnaissance: How Hackers Gather Intelligence

Like you have many tools for pen testing, hackers have many tools to probe systems, applications, networks, and more to find security vulnerabilities. An experienced and advanced hacker knows there are many more paths to enter by and is familiar with various ways to gather information and bypass security:

>> **Social engineering:** Essentially, this is when someone (knowingly or not) gives a username/password to a hacker. It's the fastest way to bypass security to this day. See the nearby sidebar and Chapter 4 for more about this issue.

>> **Spying:** The advanced hacker knows how to collect information by basically spying to learn about what security features exist to learn ways to bypass them undetected. Here are just a few examples of how a hacker might gain information that helps them simply walk through the front door undetected:

- *Dumpster diving:* Dumpster diving is the act of going through trash to find handwritten information or other printed documents with information that can be used against someone, such as login information, passwords, account information, and many other pieces of private data.

- *Screen scraping:* Screen scraping is when an application copies what it sees on a system, search engine, or other data source and makes a copy.

- *Fake covers to record credit card info:* These capture the information from your cards as you swipe them across a fake reader, which then allows a hacker to use the information it records. It looks just like an ATM machine (as an example) and you wouldn't even recognize it was a secondary cover.

Passive reconnaissance (which is somewhat like the active version) is also important to know about. Active reconnaissance testing is much like a port scan that shows you what ports may be open and what you can compromise. Passive reconnaissance is learning about and gaining knowledge through observation without actively engaging the systems you want to know about. Think of active like I'm probing a system and it's answering me; whereas with passive, I'm doing an eavesdropping attack and recording the information I'm learning about.

REMEMBER

Even though pen testing is an amazing program that allows you to gather information on weaknesses and how to prevent or fix them, it doesn't solve the entire security problem. Take that into account when you're conducting security assessments for your organization.

IN THIS CHAPTER

» Learning how to build your toolkit

» Scanning hosts on your network with Nessus

» Capturing and analyzing network data with Wireshark

» Conducting pen testing, vulnerability scanning, and forensics with Kali Linux

» Looking for hosts and services on a computer network with Nmap

Chapter **3**

Gathering Your Tools

As a pen tester, you need a set of tools that allows you to conduct assessments, scans, and tests of networks, systems, and all the devices connected to them. These tools give you the ability to test your network, systems, hosts, and devices and assess their securability.

The point is to make sure that you find the problems in your security before the hackers do. By running assessments, you can analyze the issues, assess the risks, and close them up — or at least monitor them. The best way to do this is to have a set of tools that allows you to conduct pen tests. In this chapter, I cover the most used tools and get you up and running like a pro!

Considerations for Your Toolkit

Keep these considerations in mind as you're building your toolkit:

» **The toolkit you create will be on a portable device.** A laptop or portable workstation provides you with the best outcome.

- **You need to connect to networks to conduct tests.** Your network connections should be robust, and you should have a wired as well as a wireless network interface card (NIC) or antenna.

- **It takes some time (and effort) to build a really good and high-quality toolkit.** Select the operating system you will use wisely. For example, there is a wide amount of support for Window and Apple OS; however, Linux allows for the greatest variety of tools used in their native environment. You can also set up a virtual machine to launch your tools.

- **Make sure you keep your toolkit system secure.** You don't want your tools ever used for malicious activities.

- **The tools you use and the kit you build need to be as dynamic as the attacks, threats, vulnerabilities, and issues you find along the way.** There is nothing static about information technology and all its moving parts. For example, code changes when it's upgraded to newer versions, potentially introducing bugs. Your toolkit is no different. Keep your toolkit updated and free of issue.

- **Download and set up your tools from reputable resources to avoid malware.** As an example, you might use Google to find a tool such as Nmap, and it might take you to a place where you download and install a Trojan horse application instead.

- **Look for software that has been around a long time and is owned by a reputable company.** Ideally, you want software from a company that invests time and money into the operation and upkeep of the tool and also has a great support structure. Is the software supported? If something happens, can you get help?

In the rest of this chapter, I describe reputable tools that you can easily download and will be useful throughout your pen testing careers.

Nessus

I start with Nessus because it's one of the most commonly used tools in penetration testing and you'll definitely want to get familiar with it. Figure 3-1 shows a scan that I produced from Nessus.

Nessus allows you to scan hosts on your network and the tool also lets you know whether there are concerns in the form of known risks, vulnerabilities, and exploits. (See Chapter 10 for more about these.)

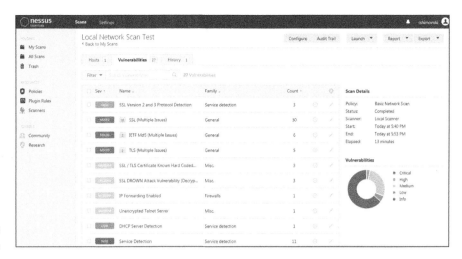

FIGURE 3-1:
Nessus output.

TIP

Nessus offers a free trial to try before you commit. Take advantage of that offer to see whether the tool suits you.

You can go to https://www.tenable.com to sign up for an account and download Nessus. Be sure to select the Nessus professional executable and select either 32- or 64-bit based on the hardware or software install you have. Tenable sends you an activation code.

Once you register and have a key, insert the key and create a set of credentials to use with the tool. This is what you use to log into your Nessus console to run scans and get reports. If you install this on a local system (such as the one you run your toolkit on), it installs as part of localhost and be accessible at https://localhost:8834.

Here's how to get started with Nessus:

1. **Open the Nessus console by going to the link provided or opening the Nessus Web Client.**

   Figure 3-2 shows the output from a scan I conducted against a network router on a local subnet.

2. **To create a new scan, select My Scans from the navigation pane on the left side of the console, and then Basic Network Scan from the template selection.**

   Over a dozen templates are available for advanced scans, cloud scans, and other types, as shown in Figure 3-3. But for now, you can stick with a Basic Network Scan.

3. **Enter your information requested such as name of scan and hosts to scan as shown in Figure 3-4.**

4. **Save your scan, close it, and retrieve it from My Scans to repeat the scan post remediation and/or when its fixed as per the risk register.**

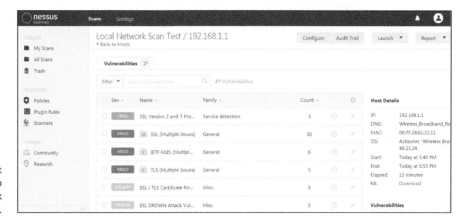

FIGURE 3-2:
Using Nessus to scan a network router.

FIGURE 3-3:
Select a scan template type.

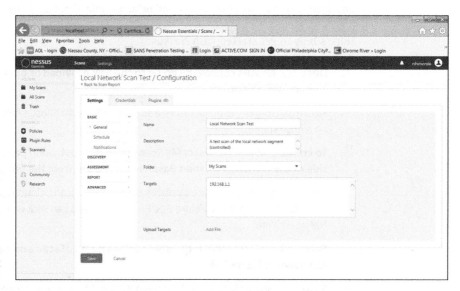

FIGURE 3-4:
Create your first Nessus scan.

Wireshark

Wireshark is a tool that can look at data and show you the various communication paths that exist — including those that are not authorized. Wireshark is one of the most powerful tools I've ever used in my entire information technology career.

You use the tool primarily to capture data from your network, so you can analyze it. You'll need to be able to decode information that you capture with it. Wireshark is good to conduct vulnerability assessments and find risks.

With this tool, your machine grabs packets promiscuously off the network where you review them. This information can be very valuable. Imagine being able to see what is traversing a network you're responsible for. As you can imagine, hackers often use this information to exploit a network and its hosts.

TIP

Although labeled a protocol analyzer, Wireshark functions as a vulnerability scanner. Its primary functions are to capture and filter traffic on a network and perform deep inspection of capture packets and protocol analysis.

The way it works is simple. It sets up your wired or wireless interface cards on your toolkit system to promiscuously sniff and capture network traffic. Figure 3-5 shows simple output from Wireshark; it clearly shows a Secure Sockets Layer (SSL) in use that is protecting the traffic.

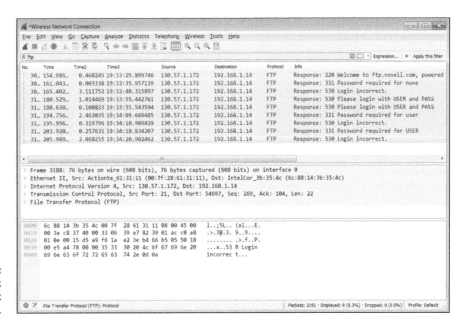

FIGURE 3-5:
Using Wireshark Network Analyzer.

To get Wireshark, go to wireshark.org and then the Download section. Select which version you'd like based on your system architecture and then follow the installation instructions. Select all defaults to include WinPcap, which is the API (application programming interface) required to install Wireshark.

To use Wireshark to run a vulnerability scan, follow these steps:

1. **Launch the Wireshark tool from your start menu.**

   The Wireshark Network Analyzer launch pad opens, as shown in Figure 3-6.

2. **Select the interface you want to use.**

   In Figure 3-6, I selected the interface that is currently passing traffic, which is the wireless network connection.

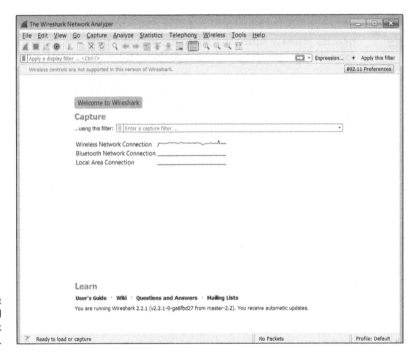

FIGURE 3-6:
Launching and using Wireshark to analyze traffic.

3. **Capture packets and then stop the capture and save it when you have collected enough information to run your review.**

   Select Start Capture from the toolbar or the Capture menu. Run the capture briefly to find what data is traversing your network.

   You can select any packet captured and drill down into it as shown in Figure 3-7.

Now you can use Wireshark for the following purposes:

» **Look at passwords and ports in use.** With the data in Figure 3-7, I can see whether any passwords were sent in cleartext. I can look at the hexadecimal output in the packet window and see it's all encrypted, leaving passwords masked away from hackers.

I can also see what ports are in use, what the source and destination IP and MAC addressing in use is, and many other details that provide clues on either a risk-free network or things I should be concerned with, such as passwords sent in cleartext. This is also known as a *password capture hack* that a Man in the Middle (MiTM) attack may produce. See Chapter 5 for more on a Man in the Middle attack.

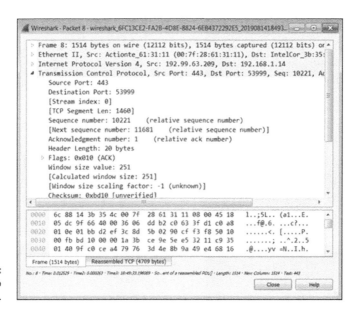

FIGURE 3-7:
Drilling down into captured data.

» **What hosts are communicating with other hosts:** I can look at the endpoints communicating back and forth, as shown in Figure 3-8. I can see whether any hosts are more in use, which are vulnerable to hackers. I can then scan them with Nessus and secure them if needed.

» **Test FTP access:** An FTP to a remote host can very quickly expose cleartext passwords if you're not careful, as shown in Figure 3-9. By conducting this test, you can quickly create a process in which all users must use Secure FTP (an encrypted FTP tool) to mitigate risk and secure your users and systems.

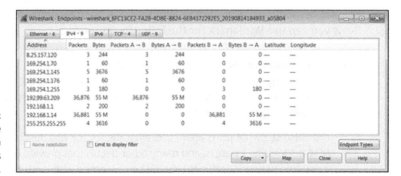

FIGURE 3-8:
Examining the traffic between host endpoints with Wireshark.

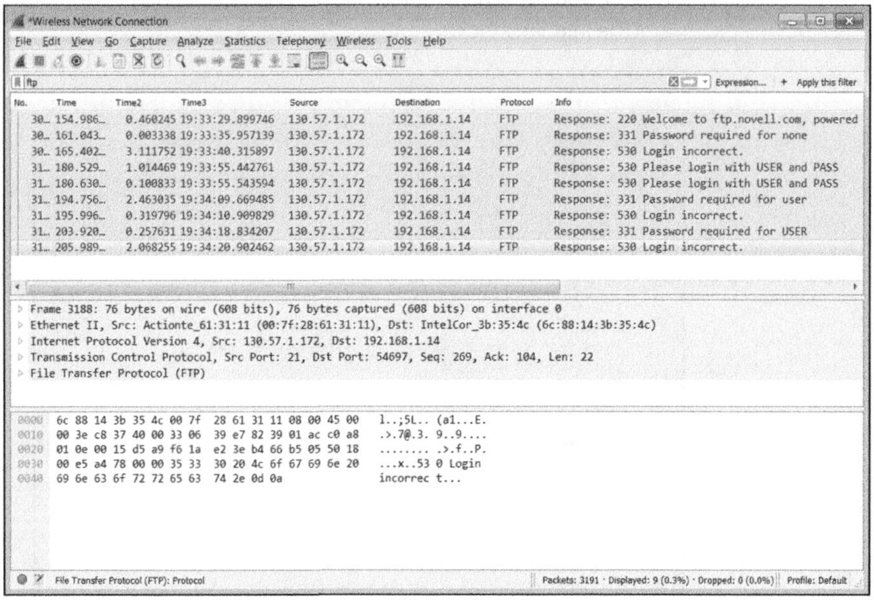

FIGURE 3-9:
Testing FTP access with Wireshark.

Kali Linux

Kali Linux is a toolset, part of a Debian-based Linux distribution, purpose-made for pen testing, vulnerability scanning, and forensics. It includes security tools (such as Aircrack-ng, Armitage, Burp suite, Cisco Global Exploiter, Ettercap, John the Ripper, Kismet, Maltego, Metasploit framework, Nmap, OWASP ZAP), social engineering tools (Sqlmap, Wireshark, Hydra), and reverse engineering tools (Binwalk, Foremost, and Volatility).

You can download it directly to your Linux install, or you can download it to a virtual machine (which is what I'm doing for the purpose of this book) from Offensive Security, which packages it with either VMware or VirtualBox software. There are directions to do either directly from kali.org based on which one you'd like.

TIP

You can install many of the tools that come with Kali independently, but I recommend installing the complete toolset. You'll use many of them.

TIP

Before you download Kali, make sure you have a system large enough to handle it and the required memory to run the applications. It generally takes more than three gigabytes to install. Kali.org recommends a minimum of 3.8GB hard disk and 2GB of RAM to install Kali.

Figure 3-10 shows a console in Kali with the preloaded tools ready to go. For this example, I have used a tool called tcdump to sniff the network traffic coming through the network to and from my source computer to multiple destinations.

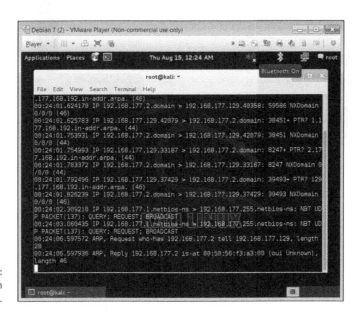

FIGURE 3-10:
Using tcdump on
Kali Linux.

WARNING

Kali is a Linux install, and it's unforgiving. Everything is case sensitive; for example, **nmap** or **tcpdump**. Typing **Nmap** or **TCPdump** is incorrect.

To start using Kali, follow these steps:

1. **Find your Kali install through the Applications menu.**

   As shown in Figure 3-11, there are top ten tools, information gathering, and sniffing/spoofing tools (like Wireshark) all found within. When you have time, be sure to explore them all.

FIGURE 3-11:
Explore the Kali
Linux toolset.

2. **Choose the Vulnerability Analysis category and then nmap.**

   Or you can open a console and type **nmap**. Nmap (short for network mapper) is a pen testing tool that allows you to find and discover hosts on the network or if you know about one, point Nmap to it so it can scan it for vulnerabilities. I cover Nmap briefly in the next section.

3. **After you run a scan of the network, examine the output.**

   Nmap lists the various open ports found on various hosts, as shown in Figure 3-12. An attacker can gain access to these ports. You can track down which should be open and which shouldn't.

For example, Port 80 is generally used for web traffic and almost always left open. Port 22 is used for Secure Shell (SSH) and is an encrypted telnet method.

TIP

To learn more about ports and see which ones are configured by default visit the iana.org website at https://www.iana.org/assignments/service-names-port-numbers/service-names-port-numbers.xhtml.

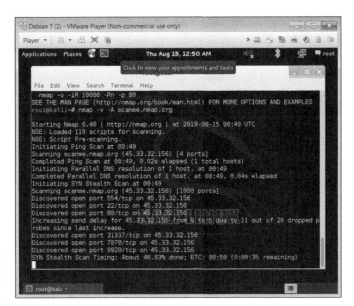

FIGURE 3-12:
Loading and using Nmap in Kali Linux.

Nmap

Nmap is a network mapper that's used to discover hosts and services on a computer network. It does so by sending packets and analyzing the responses. (You can download and install Nmap for Windows at `https://nmap.org/download.html`.) In Figure 3-13, I use an example of a possible SYN stealth scan to probe TCP ports for them to answer, thus proving a map of the network within the tool. I introduce real-world pen testing scenarios in Chapter 2 with a brief discussion of ping sweeps and how open ports can be used by hackers to gain entry into your systems.

When you finish mapping the network, you can study the topology map to find places you might want to secure from hackers who are looking for jump-off points to get around your network and into other areas or secure hosts.

REMEMBER

Hackers don't always come in from the outside through your firewall, sometimes they're sitting in cubicles inside your networking running a tool just like this looking for holes.

Note: Zenmap is Nmap — just the front-end shell to a console-based tool (as found in Kali) — to manipulate the GUI and uses Nmap on a Windows desktop. On the Nmap Output tab is the syntax used by the GUI, which you can use in the console-based Kali version to get the same effect. It's a way to dummy-proof yourself in learning the many, many ways to get Nmap to work, especially in a Linux system.

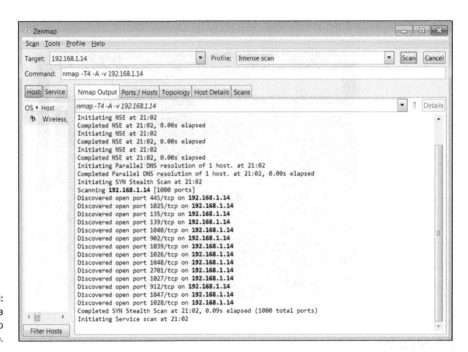

FIGURE 3-13:
Creating a
network map
with Nmap.

2

Understanding the Different Types of Pen Testing

Get at overview of attack vectors and the different types of attack types as well as encryption and cryptology.

Learn about advanced persistent threats (APT) and how they lead to other assumption attacks, such as Man in the Middle (MiTM).

Discover how attackers can overwhelm and disrupt networks with Denial of Service (DoS) and distributed denial of service (DDoS) attacks.

Explore the various types of destroy attacks — those meant to destroy a company's assets.

Go in depth with subvert attacks; they're how hackers can sneak past controls undetected.

Chapter **4**

Penetrate and Exploit

enetrate and exploit might sound like the title of an intense video game where you have to break into an enemy's fortress and expose their weakness to the world. What that means in the context of pen testing isn't too far off from that and is also intense. *Penetration* involves the attempt (perhaps successful, perhaps not) to circumvent or break through security barriers, to access a company's data, for instance. An *exploit* is when an intruder successfully penetrates the barriers and then takes advantage of a system's vulnerability.

A good part of your day as a pen tester is to think like a hacker. Where can they penetrate your systems? What information can they exploit for their own gain? This can sometimes take creative thinking!

I also discuss attack vectors in this chapter. They can be confusing to new pen testers because the bad guy hackers often know where to start their attacks, and the white hats need to figure that out. This chapter helps to demystify that by explaining client-side and server-side attacks, wireless attacks, and other points of entry into a secure location. I devote the last section of this chapter to introducing you to encryption, which can be a white hat's best friend and a black hat's enemy.

Here's the hard truth: You can't secure everything. You can't make everything bulletproof. The open nature of systems and having the ability to access resources and using them will always leave some form of hole in your security plan. What you should be aware of is that there will always be the ability to penetrate and exploit just by the basic usage of the network and its systems alone. Every time you go on the Internet and access a website (Amazon, say) to go shopping, you can also potentially launch an attack on that entity through the same exact path you used to access its services.

Understanding Vectors and the Art of Hacking

A solid understanding of how an attacker can penetrate and exploit your valuable resources is a necessity. But it's a challenge because the technology is always changing and advancing. So do the types of attacks.

For example, in the past you could set up a tight perimeter with a firewall and make sure all your internal devices were configured with antivirus protection to avoid malware attacks and be assured your network was pretty secure. Now, with wireless networks, mobile devices, the Internet of Things (IoT), cloud interfaces, and the sheer complexity of technology, a good firewall isn't enough to keep your network secure.

As we look into the future, things are going to get even more complicated. With IoT, you can imagine that just about anything and everything can and will be connected to a computer network.

The basis where all hacks start from is a vector. A *vector* (or path) of attack is how a hacker can get in. When every single device is connected to a computer network, it can be an entry point into safeguarded data or assets. The attack vector isn't only widened, it's also made deeper. Consider these vectors in regard to your networks:

>> Through your protected (or unprotected) firewalls to the Internet

>> Through a router that connects your network to the outside world (public or private)

>> From an older dialup or other out-of-band access systems in your organization

>> Through an unsecured wireless connection inside your organization

>> From a device inside the network (similar to a black box solution) running a program such as Raspberry Pi

- Someone walking through the front door of your facility and faking access to get into secure zones in your data center

- A spoofed phone call from a known source number to trick a helpdesk agent into changing a password, giving access to a system

This is just a few that you'll encounter, and I explore many other vectors throughout the book.

Constantly considering new and creative ways a hacker can attack vectors is defense in depth. Once you start thinking outside the scope of known vectors, you'll have a successful career in pen testing.

Examining Types of Penetration Attacks

Getting into a network through a password is just one way for a hacker to attack a system. A hacker can access many more vectors to penetrate a network. In the following sections, I discuss a few of them and how you can test for them.

Social engineering

Social engineering attacks are the most commonly used type of penetration attack, and yet they're the easiest to prevent with enough safeguards in place. They actually don't rely on technology at all.

All that is required in a social engineering attack is for someone — whether knowingly or tricked into it — to give a username/password to a hacker. They extract the information either by calling the employee and pretending to be an authorized person (such as an IT professional). Or they can simply set up a clone website (such as a bank website or intranet portal) that looks like the one the person is expecting. The hacker sees everything entered in the clone website, including username and password.

Then the hacker has access to everything that person has (imagine money, insider information, and any other company secrets). It's simply the easiest route a hacker can take. It takes a lot less time to trick a person into handing over a username/password than it does trying to brute-force their way through firewalls.

You can track down social engineering using Kali; you can also prevent it from happening in the first place. I discuss both in the following sections.

Using Kali to combat social engineering

You can use Kali (see Chapter 3) to root out people vulnerable to social engineering by simulating one. The Social Engineering Toolkit (SET) allows you to attack by the numbers.

One way to do this is by cloning a website to test internal end users. For example, you can clone the company's intranet where end users log in and use certain features for work. This portal may also give them access to company assets, applications, and other forms of data. If you can conduct a test and see how many end users would fall for this type of attack, you can use that information to find ways to ensure that this doesn't actually happen in your company. This may come from end user education to explain that they may see clues (perhaps in the URL itself) or other suggestions such as spoofing or a spear phishing email pointing them to it. By doing so, you may help to secure your internal assets through educating your end users. (End users can sometimes be technologies weakest link.)

Here's how to clone a site using Kali Linux:

1. **Choose Kali Linux ⇨ Exploitation Tools ⇨ Social Engineering Toolkit, as shown in Figure 4-1.**

FIGURE 4-1: Accessing the Kali Linux menu to begin a social engineering attack.

2. **Choose Social Engineering Attacks, as shown in Figure 4-2.**

3. **Choose Website Attack Vectors, as shown in Figure 4-3.**

    By choosing Website Attack Vectors, you're selecting the vector where an end user can use a website as the landing point of the spoofed attack.

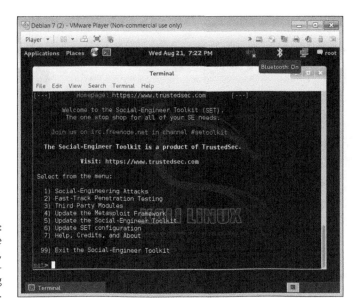

FIGURE 4-2:
From the
Toolkit menu,
choose Social-
Engineering
Attacks.

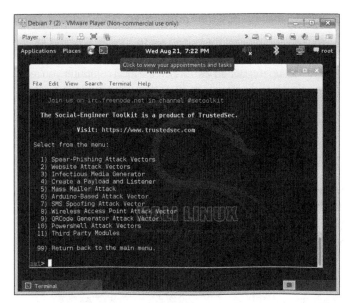

FIGURE 4-3:
Choose Website
Attack Vectors
from this list.

4. **Choose Site Cloner, as shown in Figure 4-4.**

   This option clones a site so that it appears to be the exact copy of the original.
   You can also use web templates or create a custom import; however, I'm
   keeping this example simple with a site cloner.

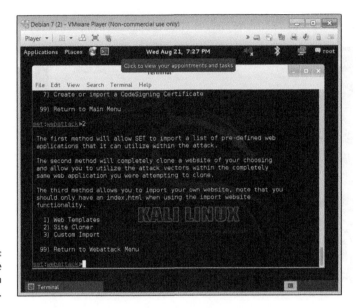

FIGURE 4-4:
Cloning a site
re-creates an
exact replica of it.

5. Select Localhost and then press Enter.

You can also redirect the cloned site to another server or location. Localhost is simply the local computer that defaults to an IP address of 127.0.0.1, meaning it will set up the cloned website on the local computer you're working on. You can set this to whatever site, IP, or host you would like if conducting this test on a different host system. Figure 4-5 shows the options I selected to get a cloned website set up.

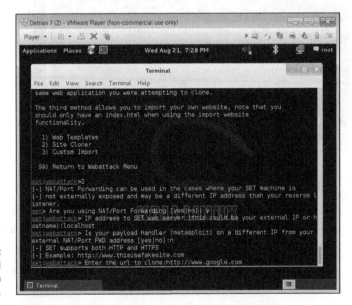

FIGURE 4-5:
The options I
chose to create a
clone website.

Now your clone website is ready. (Figure 4-6 shows how I set up a fake Google.com.)

FIGURE 4-6:
I set up a clone
Google.com —
for pen-testing
purposes only!

The purpose of the clone site is to see whether you can use it as a test in your own organizations or for your clients. If you attach this to an email and send it as a phishing attack in your organization, you can then assess how many logged into or entered data into your fake website. Log into the server hosting the site and look at how many logins or attempts you get, which can give you an idea on who is using the site and how much. You can then set up a corrective action of training for your client base.

REMEMBER

You can only use your clone website for white hat hacking or pen testing in a security vulnerability test fashion.

Preventing social engineering the non-tech way

Other ways you can prevent social engineering from happening is to ensure that there is a strict (and enforced) password protection policy in place. For example, you can configure your network security to force end users to create only hard to guess passwords and make them change passwords (and not reuse them) over a period of time. And not write them down anywhere! You can also hold mandatory education classes that help end users recognize clone websites, phishing URLs, and cold calls.

Other attempts at social engineering is from dumpster diving (which can be an actual garbage dumpster outside) but more likely the trash inside the office space itself. Having a shredder or other paper disposal unit for this purpose is essential to keeping good housekeeping and basic security in check to thwart this type of simple attack. Lastly, shoulder surfing (or keyboard surfing) is also another simple attack where someone simply observes what is typed, memorizes it, and then duplicates it.

Client-side and server-side attacks

The endpoints are the weakest areas in security (human beings are one of those endpoints). The technology they use (desktops, mobiles, laptops, tablets, and phones) are the other endpoints.

Figure 4-7 shows a very simplified view of a common network with three different segments: the segment where end users live, which is usually where the endpoints exist as well as wireless access points (WAPs) and most of the connectivity takes place; the segment where network resources such as data access via a database, network servers, virtualized servers, network attached storage, and applications live; and the segment where people gain access to the outside world via a firewall, network router, private or public links such as the Internet, and access to other data and applications via cloud resources.

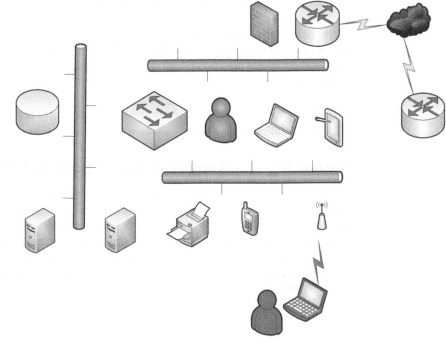

FIGURE 4-7: The different areas of attack vectors.

Viewing a simple network such as this, you can see where a network attacker or hacker can gain access to any of it from inside the network and sometimes from outside of the network. Your job is to test all these exploits, try to penetrate all of these resources, and if you do gain access, shore it up before a hacker gains access to the vector.

A list of access points includes (but not limited to):

>> **From the outside in:** The ability to penetrate a firewall is extremely difficult. One of the ways attackers try to gain access into a computer network is via router hopping from routers they can access outside of your network (perhaps in your ISP) and through to your DMZ (*demilitarized zone,* any external-facing area of your network that is exposed to untrusted networks) and into your private and protected internal network.

   This is the hardest way and inconsequently it's also the most monitored via a company's security operations team. To pen test this area, I would suggest external scans to the edge and all access points from the outside of the network in. I would also suggest testing your ISP and working with it to make sure that it's also running penetration tests on its network systems.

>> **The inside or internal network:** You can conduct a pen test using tools such aa Nmap to map the inside network and see what is available and accessible. I introduce Nmap in Chapter 3.

>> **The inside wireless network:** This is the most likely attack vector because it's usually left open for ease of use. Many companies run parallel SSIDs (and networks) where inside resources are controlled and secured and those just looking to gain access to the Internet with a BYOD (*Bring Your Own Device,* a scenario in which employees use personal devices — phones, laptops, tablets, and so on — to access company assets) may use the open unsecured wireless network.

>> **Malware:** Malware (or malicious software) are other forms of software that implants trojans, backdoors, open ports, worms, and bugs inside your systems that allows others to connect remotely and exploit systems. Running pen tests (scans) and identifying open listening ports and other various holes can help to find these types of issues rather quickly.

>> **Endpoints:** Privilege escalation on Windows systems is a common one where software is installed or bugs are found in drivers and other pieces of software that allows an attacker to gain access to trusted areas of the operating system.

>> **Users:** This is one of the hardest vectors to deal with because it may be one of your most senior technical assets abusing their power and privilege. In these cases, it's helpful to have a separation of duties and in some cases, random auditing, accounting, and the ability to capture logs via authentication that allows these types of attack vectors to be monitored and handled if abused.

This list is by no means exhaustive. It's simply enough to get you started and hopefully thinking that penetration testing needs to be done in all vectors so that you can identify the many possibly entry points into your systems, data, and assets.

Password cracking

All interconnected devices need to communicate and almost every single one of them requires an account so human beings can access and use them. Other services can sit over them (think enterprise management software) and overlay the management of them with a bigger tool. Either way, they require accounts to be managed, and accounts require credentials — a username and a password.

Despite the warnings over the years, people still use obvious and easy-to-guess passwords for their systems (such as the names of their children or pets). And because usernames are usually some version of first initial and last name (or other common variation) with the company's domain name as the second portion, old school hackers can easily gain access by just guessing at the logon credentials.

Fortunately, many systems are set up to require strong passwords (passwords using upper and lowercase, numbers, special characters), and for them to be changed on a routine basis. But hackers still have a fairly easy way to get in through password cracking.

Password cracking is accomplished through a tool that attempts all possible username and password combinations using a dictionary file. With enough time, the correct username/password combination is usually found. This can be done locally or done remotely via tools (such as Kali and Metasploit). Figure 4-8 shows an example of a password cracking attack with Metasploit Pro.

```
[+] [2019.08.22-10:20:25] Workspace:Test Scan Progress:2187/2187 (100%) Complete (0 sessions opened, 11 hosts targeted, 0 hosts skipped)
[+] [2019.08.22-10:20:26] Workspace:Test Scan Progress:1/2 (50%) Cracking weak passwords found during collection...
[*] [2019.08.22-10:20:27] Wordlist file written out to C:/Windows/Temp/jtrtmp20190822-3320-1t339vi
[*] [2019.08.22-10:20:28] Hashes Written out to C:/Windows/Temp/hashes_tmp20190822-3320-ppxiup
[*] [2019.08.22-10:20:28] Cracking lm hashes in normal wordlist mode...
[*] [2019.08.22-10:20:29] No password hashes loaded (see FAQ)
[*] [2019.08.22-10:20:29] Cracking lm hashes in single mode...
[*] [2019.08.22-10:20:29] No password hashes loaded (see FAQ)
[*] [2019.08.22-10:20:29] Cracking lm hashes in incremental mode (All4)...
[*] [2019.08.22-10:20:29] No password hashes loaded (see FAQ)
[*] [2019.08.22-10:20:29] Cracking lm hashes in incremental mode (Digits)...
[*] [2019.08.22-10:20:30] No password hashes loaded (see FAQ)
[*] [2019.08.22-10:20:30] Cracked Passwords this run:
[*] [2019.08.22-10:20:30] Cracking nt hashes in normal wordlist mode...
[*] [2019.08.22-10:20:30] No password hashes loaded (see FAQ)
[*] [2019.08.22-10:20:30] Cracking nt hashes in single mode...
[*] [2019.08.22-10:20:30] No password hashes loaded (see FAQ)
[*] [2019.08.22-10:20:30] Cracking nt hashes in incremental mode (Digits)...
[*] [2019.08.22-10:20:30] No password hashes loaded (see FAQ)
[*] [2019.08.22-10:20:30] Cracked Passwords this run:
[+] [2019.08.22-10:20:30] Workspace:Test Scan Progress:2/2 (100%) Obtained 0 loots; Found 0 creds; Cracked 0 new hashes
```

FIGURE 4-8:
A password crack
via Metasploit.

REMEMBER

This kind of attack is exactly why security professional implore people to change their passwords on a regular basis. With enough time (and computers have all the time in the world), usernames and passwords can be hacked. If passwords are changed, it lessens the chance that a computer will hit on the right combination of letters, numbers, and special characters.

Cryptology and Encryption

One of the most common attacks is password cracking, and the use of encryption can thwart many of the tools I discuss in this chapter. Keep the following points in mind as you dive into how encryption works:

>> *Encryption* is the process in which you have cleartext data that you run through a protected cipher; this produces a key to *decrypt* (decode) the data. You want to protect the key, so when you transmit the data, only the recipient can decode and use it.

>> *Cryptology* is the study and work done with encryption methods. Many consider it to be one of the hardest parts of learning about security because it's complex and confusing.

>> Although you need to understand many concepts about encryption to exploit them, you can let the tool handle most of the work to run a pen test on encryption. Then you can view the reports to get an understanding of what the tool found and what risks you need to mitigate.

>> I cover some of the most common forms of encryption here at a very high level of how they are used and their practicality when running pen tests. This is not an all-inclusive discussion because encryption, the math involved, and all of the different ways it's implemented could fill a 300-page book (at least).

>> If you are new to encryption, use this chapter to run the tools and reports. Later, you can study things as they start to appear in your reports. This gives you a springboard to learning more about encryption and its methods.

Security analysts and pen testers like to use the CIA (confidentiality, integrity, and availability) triad to model security operations using encryption. By using this model, you can design any form of security using encryption whether you're securing data in transit or data at rest.

When you transform data with encryption (typically done with a transform set), it hides and makes the data. Figure 4-9 shows that while accessing a website that is protected by encryption, all communications sent through are encrypted and can't be read in cleartext if data is captured and reviewed.

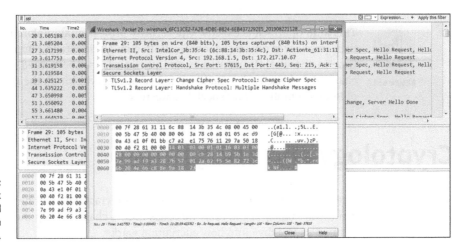

FIGURE 4-9:
Using Wireshark to capture and expose data protected by SSL.

As a pen tester, encryption is a great way to show that you aren't at risk by someone simply running a packet capture tool, grabbing some network traffic, and picking out information that gives them access to your network. This is why encryption is so important.

SSL/TLS

Secure Sockets Layer (SSL) is a protocol that provides encryption, an authentication method, and provides message integrity. It comes in different bit strengths and the bit strength denotes how secure it is. For example, 40-bit encryption is not as strong as 128-bit encryption (SSL 3.0). Tools such as Metasploit or Nessus help you identify weak versions of encryption.

Transport Layer Security (TLS) is an open-community standard that provides many of the same services as SSL. It's more extensible and more commonly used in today's infrastructures. SSL and TLS are used when data is in transit (not at rest).

SSH

Many older systems still have a telnet daemon or service running that allows an attacker to begin a password cracking attack. A *secure shell* (SSH) is the stronger replacement for telnet.

It's an application and protocol that is used to remotely log in to another computer using a secure tunnel and allows you to secure data (much like SSL does) in transit from being captured and used through encryption. A session key is exchanged from the computer requesting a connection to the computer you want to connect with, and this builds the secure channel between them.

IPsec

The *Internet Protocol Security* (IPsec) protocol also builds secure channels between devices using a Virtual Private Network (VPN). VPNs are used to create a tunnel between a sender and a receiver so that data in transit can be secured with encryption. Specific algorithms and cryptographic keys are required for IPsec to work and it can be complicated to configure. Most of the time, this type of encryption is set up on network devices looking to communicate with other network devices to share information, such as routing updates, tables, and adjacency information. It commonly uses pre-shared keys to credentials to build secure connections.

Using Metasploit Framework and Pro

Metasploit is a tool maintained by Rapid7 (`rapid7.com`). You can download a free trial for Linux or Windows and get it up and running pretty easily for test and use within minutes. If you want to learn the tool and run your first pen test with it, simply sign up for an account by accessing the free trial links. You'll get a copy of Metasploit Pro for download; install it (an easy process), and then request a trial key via the login interface where you set up the tool.

Before I get into the specifics of using this tool, a few words of caution:

» **Be patient.** Depending on your network segment and what options you select, the pen test can take some time.

» **Do not scan without permission.** Make sure you're conducting an ethical hack/pen test and that you not only have permission but have created awareness about it with key IT personnel.

This way if something goes wrong, you can stop the scan and assess the damage and correct it. Even when you take precautions, scans cause issues at times, especially on a production network.

» **Always monitor a scan.** Scanning and walking away isn't recommended because you may identify a critical risk that needs to be assessed (and perhaps corrected) immediately. It should also be monitored by security operations analysts for this reason alone.

» **Keep your tools up to date.** The Metasploit Administration menu has a software update option (in the top-right corner of the dashboard).

» **Back up any critical data before you scan.** You'll want to back up data on hosts you think might be corrupted or otherwise negatively impacted by the scan.

Follow these steps to run a scan with Metasploit Pro:

1. **Access Metasploit on your local system by going to the URL set up for you during the installation process:**

   ```
   https://localhost:3790/
   ```

2. **Log in and click the Quick PenTest link.**

   The Quick PenTest wizard shown in Figure 4-10 opens.

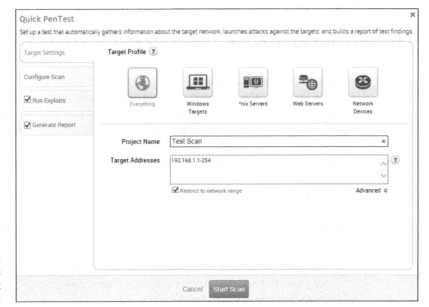

FIGURE 4-10:
Metasploit Pro's
Quick PenTest
wizard.

3. **Choose a target profile, give your project a name, and enter the Target Addresses.**

   You can choose the Everything option, which takes longer to conduct, or specific targets, such as Windows Targets.

   At this prompt I left all of the defaults and added a project name and a target address to scan. This tool has some intelligence to start with a default scan of the local subnet you're attached to based on your IP address. Here it captured a small private addressing range of 192.168.1.0/24. It allows for the scanning of 254 hosts on the subnet.

4. **Click Start Scan.**

   Figure 4-11 shows the scan as it runs. One of the tools it starts with is a network mapping service with Nmap.

Once the scan completes and the segment is mapped, the tool then probes, tests, and runs a series of vulnerability tests and other services to get a complete picture of the segments risks and what can be exploited.

5. **When the scan is complete, access the findings by viewing the output on the Metasploit console window and buffer or in logs.**

   When you complete your scanning and assessment, you'll review reports and findings to see what you need to fix, monitor or add to a risk register. I cover findings, reporting, and determining next steps in Part 4.

FIGURE 4-11:
Running a quick pen test with Metasploit Pro.

REMEMBER

Your toolkit leverages some of the same tools found in other aspects of your toolset. For example, having Kali in your toolkit includes Nmap. Having Metasploit in Kali includes Nmap. You can also use Nmap by itself as a standalone tool, which I show in Chapter 3.

I showed you a Windows version outside of Kali Linux, so you can get in the habit of seeing pen test tools being used on both a Windows and Linux system. This way, no matter what you decide to use as a toolkit (Linux native, Windows, or a VMware or Virtual Box host), you'll be ready to scan! Using the tools on either platform is a nearly identical process, so you can mix and match. That said, if you wanted to run Metasploit from Kali, you can do that from the Exploitation Tools menu.

IN THIS CHAPTER

» Conducting web vulnerability scans
with Burp Suite

» Using Wireshark to get in the middle
of network conversations

» Collecting data via devious means:
spoofing, eavesdropping, key logging,
and more

Chapter **5**

Assumption (Man in the Middle)

I n Chapter 4, I show you how to use a toolkit and get started as a pen tester specifically in penetration and exploitation. That's a fundamental of pen testing
and when you scan for weakness and vulnerabilities, how to view them as a risk
to remediate.

Here I cover different attack types based on vector. Knowing the different attack
types is essential so that you can be more familiar with the pathways and how to
conduct these tests yourself. The goal of any hacker is to gain access to systems
and servers. Your goal as a pen tester is to thwart all hackers — or at least deter
them as much as possible — so they walk away with minimal or unusable information. The way to do that is to think like a hacker. If you wear the white hat (or
grey) you can ethically hack and exploit systems — with permission of course!

It all starts with foothold into an environment and can expand all the way to a very
in-depth series of attacks, such as an APT. With an advanced persistent threat
(APT), which is the gateway to other attacks, that foothold can become a propped
open door so you can see how deep you can penetrate and exploit.

The APT can be the gateway because after a hacker is inside and laying undetected, conducting an attack such as Man in the Middle (MiTM) is nothing more
than lying in wait. It can also lead to address spoofing (an attacker takes over the

identity of an authorized person to gain control), replay attacks (replaying credentials to gain access), and simply eavesdropping.

In this chapter, I show you how attackers conduct these kind of assumption attacks and how you can either duplicate the attack as a pen test or use the tools in the toolkit to find them and expose them.

REMEMBER

The more you're familiar with these kinds of attacks, the easier you can find them through assessment and can fix the issues. See Chapter 10 for assessment tips and prevention measures.

Toolkit Fundamentals

As a pen tester you need a solid understanding of how attackers operate and how potential attacks occur. In this section, I point out a few items you need to make sure that your system, identity, session, or other form of communications are not assumed by an attacker.

Many of these tools — such as Kali, Nessus, Wireshark — should be in your toolkit. See Chapter 3 if you still need to get your toolkit in order.

REMEMBER

What makes assumption attacks so difficult to detect is that when they're pulled off correctly, the hackers act like a pen tester, security analyst, or the CEO of the company! They can infiltrate quickly and be gone before you know there was a breach. For this reason, the lessons learned will highlight the need to harden (fortify) systems as the best form of defense against these types of attacks. See Chapter 10, where I discuss assessing what you learn from conducting test attacks and how to prevent the different types of attack.

Burp Suite

Burp Suite by portswigger.net is a web security pen testing tool that allows you to conduct web vulnerability scans as well as other types of scans to identify issues with cross site scripting (XSS), SQL injection, cross site request forgery (CSRF), and other advanced web attacks. It also uses the Burp Proxy, shown in Figure 5-1, that allows you to capture and intercept all requests sent and responses received between a web browser and a target system or application to conduct session hijacking and eavesdropping attacks.

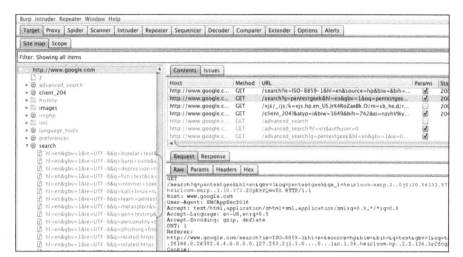

FIGURE 5-1:
Using Burp Suite
for pen testing.

In this section, I keep the examples simple, but you can customize Burp Proxy for more complex scenarios. For example, you can have it generate certificates and sign from its internal Certification (or Certificate) Authority (CA).

Burp Suite generates the tests that show how vulnerable your web architecture is. Web architecture (say, the Amazon's shopping cart) consists of three tiers:

>> **Tier 1:** This is client facing and generally called web and is exactly as it sounds: You access a web page as a client and browse the web.

>> **Tier 2 (or N tier):** This is the middleware tier where many of the cross-connection technology exists such as COM and COM+ components, applications functions, and other software that provides functionality to the web access layer and helps to further connect users to the database tier. For example, in a shopping cart, the actual shopping cart software may reside on the middleware.

Some applications have architectures that collapse or expand into other tiers; those are called *N-tier* architecture. N is any number more than 2.

>> **Tier 3:** This tier is where the databases for all transactions are stored and conducted. It's where an attacker finds the most useful information, such as credit card numbers, account information, and other valuable data.

Figure 5-2 shows this tier architecture. Using Burp Suite or other pen testing tool, you can start to see where an advanced persistent threat (APT) attack, MiTM attack, or other assumption, can be very valuable for both parties. For the attacker who gains access, there's a treasure trove of valuables to acquire. The pen tester might just be able to find the weaknesses before the hacker does.

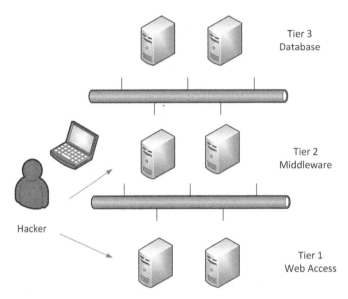

FIGURE 5-2:
Viewing an N-tier
application.

Tier 3
Database

Tier 2
Middleware

Hacker

Tier 1
Web Access

With Burp Suite, you can set up a proxy that allows you to test your web architecture by routing all web traffic through it. You can then conduct an MiTM scenario
that allows you to capture (and further analyze) all traffic back and forth to find
any weaknesses, looking for areas where hackers have the potential to conduct
replay attacks, eavesdrop, data gather, and find injection. After you have this
information, your next step is to tighten security. You can find out more about
hardening in Part 4 of this book.

WARNING

If you can get Burp Suite running to run these pen tests you have encountered one
issue. Can a hacker do the same? If you then run it and find weaknesses, you have
a second problem to address, which is the culmination of a report on the weaknesses that are found.

TIP

Other advanced attacks you can find using the Burp Suite tool are SQL injection
attacks, cross-site scripting (XSS), fuzzing attacks, and others. A tool such as
Burp Suite really focuses on these areas in particular, so if you're conducting more
advanced level tests on web applications, Burp Suite can help you identify those
threats more easily.

Wireshark

Vectors, paths and places where hackers can exploit a weakness, are just as important as the penetration itself. Wireshark gives you the ability to find vulnerable
vectors. (See Chapter 3 to find out about everything you can do with Wireshark.)
Figure 5-3 shows how a hacker can use Wireshark to divert legitimate traffic from
the user (victim) to the server or resource being used.

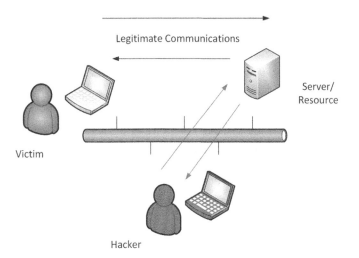

Legitimate Communications

Server/
Resource

Victim

Hacker

FIGURE 5-3:
Using Wireshark
to pen test.

The gateway to more advanced level attacks is gaining access in the first place. Because of this, you need to see firsthand what gaining access from the vector of network access can provide you.

Consider the scenario shown in Figure 5-3. You're either playing the role of hacker or pen tester. How can you connect to the network to get in the middle of this conversation? The picture is actually simplified. Quite a few steps need to take place for that to happen. Here are some key considerations to think about before you pen test:

>> You need to have a computer with Wireshark installed. This is likely the system you use with your pen test toolkit on it. This way you have your tools available to test with.

>> You need to connect to the network that the systems you want to interrupt and the data you want to intercept is riding on.

>> You need to connect to the network in a way where you can be undetected and remain so. You might want to assume the IP address of a computer (IP spoofing), so you can appear to be the victim and or the resource based on the vector of your attack.

>> You can run Wireshark and have a network interface card (or NIC) running in promiscuous mode, so you can capture all traffic on the network, not just the traffic intended to be sent to you. You need to do this in a switched environment where the communications are controlled.

>> You can run the capture on a computer and have enough space to capture the data on your toolkit system. The only alternative to this is to know exactly when the communication will take place to shorten the capture or set up a

capture filter with the specific details of the source and or destination IPs that will send and receive traffic.

>> You need to filter for and isolate the communications to review the captured data.

>> You can set up new tests (or hacks) based on what you previously captured.

In the next sections, I show you how the tools in your toolkit can be used to conduct a series of tests that allow you to find weaknesses and mitigate the risk (or at least know that they exist and assume the risk).

Listening In to Collect Data

Spoofing, eavesdropping, key logging, card skimming, and even USB drives are all ways hackers use to attack an organization for the purpose of collecting data. In this section, I talk about these various attacks and ways you can test for them.

Address spoofing

Spoofing an address is the best way to gain access in and be in the middle of a conversation. If I pretend to be you and you start to communicate with me, then I have successfully conducted a Man in The Middle (MiTM) attack. This information is vital to the pen tester. Knowing that it may require you to test one level of security first to ensure that the next level is or is not at risk makes you better at knowing what to check and when. This provides you with a foundation in how an advanced persistent attack is conducted, but also how you can conduct an advanced pen test.

The concept of spoofing is when someone can pretend to be someone they are not based on faking a digital identity. Much like identity theft in real life, the digital version is very much the same. For example, as a computer I need an IP address to be able to communicate on the network with other systems and resources, connect to the Internet, access web pages, and more.

TECHNICAL STUFF

A more technical explanation of spoofing is that an IP address spoofing attack is when an attack incepts the conversation by sending IP packets (network data that is transmitted) from a fake source address so that the recipient believes they're speaking to the real source but instead is speaking (transmitting data) with a hacker.

Some of the biggest attacks in history were difficult to identify because they all came from spoofed addresses. For example, a Denial of Service (DoS) attack is when an attacker sends an inordinate amount of traffic to a receiver in hopes of overwhelming it (the network buffers), so the system can't function correctly. The receiver has to process every network packet it receives, interrupt the CPU, and process the request, so sending tons of bogus requests simply blocks the capability for real requests to be processed in a timely fashion (if at all). Experienced hackers run this attack from a *zombie* (a computer infected with a virus that does the work for them) or from a machine that pretends to be from a place of origin that it isn't (because it's spoofed). This way, a security analyst investigating the attack can capture some of the traffic and investigate it but will discover they can't track the source of the attack because the hacker is using a fake address. See Chapter 6 for more about overwhelm and DoS attacks.

You must know how a spoof is conducted, even as you accept that it's very difficult to stop or track it. Here are a few thoughts on helping to prevent spoof attacks:

>> **Use encryption to help safeguard digital identities.** This helps to block the transmission of useable data to be captured by a packet capture device and be usable. I discuss encryption further in Chapter 4.

>> **Deploy security that doesn't allow unauthorized connections to the network.** An attacker needs to connect to the network to conduct the attack, so using tools such as Forescout (forescout.com), allows those who connect without authorization to be quarantined or examined. This is called *network access control* (NAC).

>> **Run the attacks yourself.** And then pen test the ability to conduct this attack — this gives you information about the likelihood of black hat hackers to successfully conduct this attack against you.

TECHNICAL STUFF

Other advanced attacks in which you can conduct spoofing (or the testing of spoofing) is with arp-poisoning. Regarding the OSI model and its associated layers, IP addresses operate at layer 3. The data link layer is layer 2 and where MAC addresses function. The arp cache of a machine is where the layer 2 and layer 3 addresses are mapped. If I can poison the arp cache (alter it to make changes such as spoofing), I can conduct the same attack as the IP spoofing attack.

Eavesdropping

Eavesdropping (also known as *sniffing*) is a very simple attack (and pen test) to do. After you know how to use a tool like Wireshark and can connect to a network, you simply run the tool and start to collect and gather information — that is, you eavesdrop on what's happening in hopes of sniffing out any data you can use.

Now, you want to place the tool where you believe relevant data can be collected. For example, if I know that I can sniff out data on a network segment where credentials are being used in *cleartext* (unencrypted combinations of usernames and passwords), then simple eavesdropping allows me to collect all the information I need to conduct a new attack.

Figure 5-4 shows Wireshark being used to grab the packets as they go by. You can then filter by protocol, or even by IP address, and start combing through the data to find what is relevant.

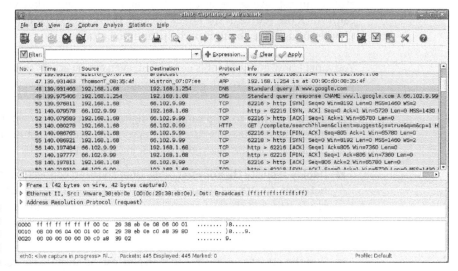

Eavesdropping as a pen tester is as simple as the attack is:

1. Set up your Wireshark packet capture tool in a place where you want to test security.

2. Run the tool and begin collecting data.

3. Use the data you capture to simulate an end user connecting to a resource, like a server, and logging in.

If you can collect enough data in Step 2 to log into a system successfully in Step 3, you know that hardening techniques (which I discuss in Chapter 10) are required to shore up your defenses.

Packet capture and analysis

Part of being a great security analyst is to have deep knowledge of networking technologies and protocols. The best way to gain that knowledge is through protocol analysis from the packet captures you can do with a tool like Wireshark.

Many network tools on the market allow for the analysis, threat detection, and management of network traffic based on how protocols operate. Using Wireshark is a very manual way of doing this and why it's a great tool for a pen tester. Packet capture is simple: You set up the tool, position it correctly, and run it to nab the packets.

The analysis portion is what really brings pen testing full circle. Successfully analyzing what you capture — determining, for example, whether a communication between a web client and its associated web server is safe and why or why not — is what you should be mastering as a pen tester. See Chapter 10 for more about doing the post-test analysis.

Key loggers

A *key logger* allows an attacker to record what keys you tap on the keyboard. It's either a device placed on a computer or a piece of software installed on it (sometimes via USB stick). After the device or software is live on your computer, the attacker can watch what you do. It's a great way to collect information such as usernames and passwords.

You'll want to test to make sure key loggers aren't live on the computers under your care. I recommend also ensuring your company has policy and tools in place to keep key loggers from being put on computers in the first place. The policy can be one that users must read and follow so that they know to add these devices or it can be an electronic policy applied to the system that can prevent any types of devices from being added without system administrator approval.

Card skimmers

A *card skimmer* is placed over a device to sit in the middle of a transmission where it can collect data. It's hidden in plain sight because it's made to look like a natural part of whatever machine it's placed on, as shown in Figure 5-5. Card skimmers are commonly used in ATM machines. The skimmer sits on the dock where the debit card is placed. Users unknowingly continue to use the ATM and their information is collected, stolen, and used. A pen tester can scan these systems to make sure these devices aren't installed.

FIGURE 5-5:
A card skimmer
on an ATM.

USB drives

Other advanced attacks take place through a very unknown vector, which is the USB drive. A hacker, criminal, or other nefarious person can place a USB stick (also known as a thumb or jump drive) in your computer and be in the middle of your business. Tools such as Sophos (sophos.com) install software that blocks usage of the USB drive and requires enhanced security measures to use the drive. I recommend scanning for this at an enterprise level to make sure that all desktop computers and laptops have this function protected or disabled.

Chapter **6**

Overwhelm and Disrupt (DoS/DDoS)

The series of attacks I cover in this chapter revolves around overwhelming targets. In previous chapters, you learn how to use specific tools to knock on the front door (or try the back door) and see if you could gain access. In this chapter, I show you how to kick in the front door.

In these scenarios, the attacker is focused on literally *overwhelming* the target to cause it to either crash, not accept real connections for service, clog up the pipes, incapacitate the system by using up all its resources, and just plain disrupt everything to cause a denial of service. I talk specifically about Denial of Service (DoS) attacks, which are unfortunately common.

I also show you how attackers (and pen testers) handle the disruption of resources through attacks such as a DoS, DDoS (distributed form of a DoS), buffer overflow attacks, and more. I discuss what tools you use to identify both whether you're experiencing a DoS attack and whether your systems are vulnerable to experiencing them. This is another fundamental of vulnerability testing and when you scan for weakness how to view them as a risk to remediate.

WARNING

You can potentially crash the systems you're testing and potentially corrupt them. Make sure that you run these tests on a test environment that duplicates the actual production environment to see not only the anticipated outcomes, but also what can't be anticipated. For example, you might send traffic to a server resource to test it only to cause it to freeze, blue screen, crash, or lock up. You might be forced to hard boot the system (or it will do it on its own), which can cause you to lose data, corrupt system files, or render the system in need of an image repair. Run these tests with great caution.

In this chapter, I show you the biggest vectors are outside and inside your network. External attacks are more prevalent in this arena, but many viruses (malware) can be circulated within your network to accomplish the same attack. The threat can be worse when you have malware in your organization that turns your own workstations into *zombies* (computers taken over by hackers) and therefore into the source of an attack.

As a pen tester, you won't launch DDoS attacks against networks. However, black hats use this technique as a way to find a vulnerability to exploit. Be cautious if you want to use this tactic because it can cause severe outages on your production network.

Toolkit Fundamentals

For overwhelm and disrupt attacks, tools such as Nmap, Kali, and even network console tools from your workstation can be used to launch an attack. You want to run all these as part of your vulnerability scanning so that you can assess whether you have weaknesses in these areas.

Make no mistake, just about every company connected to the public Internet is exposed to overwhelm and disrupt attacks.

First you use many of the tools in your toolkit, including some from Kali, Nessus, Wireshark (all of which I introduce in Chapter 3), and others to identify these attacks. What makes this particular attack extra vicious, however, is that it can be hard to identify without looking at your firewalls and routers in the network to see inbound and outbound traffic patterns.

Kali

Kali (see Chapter 3 for an overview) is useful to overwhelm and disrupt normal traffic patterns, overwhelm healthy resources, and send traffic to resources in a way that disrupts normal operation. Open Kali and navigate to the Stress Testing tools and select the Network Stress Testing menu. Over a dozen tools can help you find these vulnerabilities.

You can use a Kali tool called Inundator to run stress tests in your environment to see how your systems respond. In Figure 6-1, Inundator is sending massive amounts of traffic to hosts. The Inundator tool is a multi-threaded, queue-driven, anonymous, intrusion detection tool that generates false positives with support for multiple targets. It sends traffic to cause alerts to appear and inundate (overwhelm and disrupt normal operations) your security infrastructure, such as firewalls, routers, intrusion detection tools, and prevention gear. The inundation fills your logs and over-utilizes your resources.

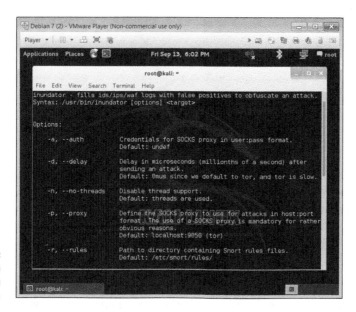

FIGURE 6-1:
Using Kali for pen testing disruption attacks.

If you're running websites from your company and you host them in your environment behind your firewall, your firewall might be intelligent enough to identify when this type of attack is taking place and either alert you or block it. Regardless, the example shows how the larger landscape is exposed.

If a hacker uses a tool such as Inundator to overwhelm your firewalls and other devices you rely on to detect attacks as they occur, you can see the pattern of a larger scale attack. A larger scale attack should be very concerning. Part of mitigating the issue is to patch your systems accordingly, remove unneeded services or open ports, and/or block these types of attacks from being able to reach your intended hosts.

Figure 6-2 shows how a hacker (or you as an ethical hacker) can launch an attack from outside of the network. In this example, I am showing a very simple design where the attacker probes your visible address space (maybe the hosted server resources via your firewall) of any and all associated devices available to scan.

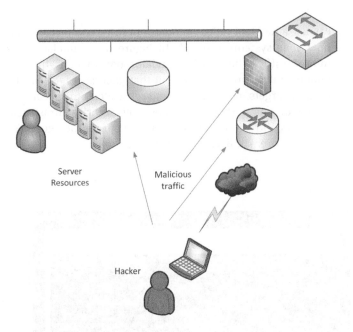

FIGURE 6-2:
Launching an
attack from
outside the
network.

Server
Resources

Malicious
traffic

Hacker

Running tools such as Nessus can do this very easily. Once I have something to work with (an address or hostname), I can then begin to send traffic to it in hopes of overwhelming it. Note that the attack can originate either from a spoofed address or from a zombie installed by malware. In any case, the attacker sends traffic to whatever external identity they can find for your network.

They can attack in so many ways. For example, part of information-gathering attacks is to map the network. In Chapter 3, I introduce Nmap and the importance of seeing how easily it is to map your internal and external networks. If you host services from your company, your public IP address space is known — which means you must protect it and monitor it for attacks.

TIP

This exact example is also how pen testers would test their internal and external network and system resources. To do the internal vulnerability assessment, simply perform the same attacks from inside (instead of outside) your network.

WARNING

Inside threats are more worrisome than outside threats. Usually, inside threats come from within your organization when trusted users, resources, and access are not fully protected. Watch this attack vector very closely.

Kali T50 Mixed Packet Injector tool

The Kali T50 Mixed Packet Injector tool is another weapon in your arsenal against overwhelm and disrupt attacks. Figure 6-3 shows the T50 tool being used by the hacker to send a flood attack to a host.

FIGURE 6-3: Using Kali T50 to send a flood attack to a host.

I am showing you how to overwhelm your systems with tools, but you must then examine those systems to identify whether they are in fact being overwhelmed. In Figure 6-4, I show you how to do just that.

When you run T50 to stress your host or hosts, you can then go to the host individually and look at the system resources:

» Windows users can look at the Windows Task Manager tool to view CPU and other system processes and start/stop them as needed.

» The Linux console provides the same information with the use of ps tools and the top command.

Here, I ran the T50 tool (you can see it running as the top-most intensive process using 94% of the CPU). Once I terminated the pen test, the CPU dropped to a normal percentage.

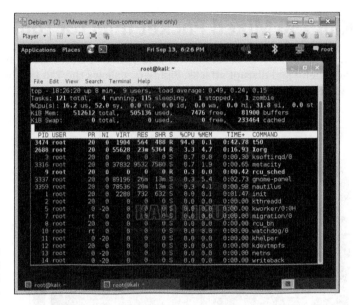

FIGURE 6-4:
Viewing resources with the Linux top command.

Understanding Denial of Service (DoS) Attacks

Denial of Service (DoS) attacks are quite simply the launch of any attack that stops legitimate services from being provided. This can be anything from the websites you host, the printers in a print room, or a wireless access point (WAP). The larger scale version of this type of attack is the DDoS, or distributed denial of service. While a DoS attack typically uses just one computer and one Internet connection to flood a targeted system or resource, the DDoS uses multiple computers and Internet connections to flood the target.

DoS is the best way to ruin not only a company's reputation, but it can also be very costly. If a good DoS attack is launched systematically against a high-level resource target (for example, a key backbone Internet router), the payload of that attack could take down half the Internet until it's resolved.

Figure 6-5 shows the attack vector and how it's conducted. In this classic case of a DDoS attack, the hacker has successfully turned zombies (workstations they've taken control of) into attack machines. This is usually done by distributing a virus (normally a downloadable Trojan horse) that turns systems unknowingly into traffic generators. The hacker can then backdoor (usually via rootkit) control these systems so that they can then launch attacks (much like flood) at anything the hacker desires.

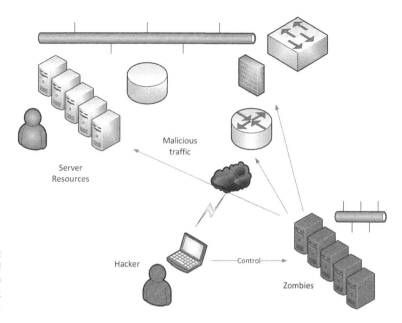

FIGURE 6-5:
How a distributed
denial of service
(DDoS) attack
works.

Server
Resources

Malicious
traffic

Hacker

Control

Zombies

When overwhelming hosts, the most common outcome from this type of attack is denial of legitimate use of the system by others. I have said for many years that information technology resources are available to be used. If you can't use them, you shouldn't have them. That said, DoS attacks are the most common because they're easiest to conduct (especially by script kiddies).

They're also the hardest to track if the overwhelming of resources is done with infected zombies. Even the best forensic teams who do incident response on these types of attacks are commonly left scratching their heads as to what could have caused them.

Regardless, you have ways to identify when this attack is taking place, which depends on which components you're viewing:

>> If you run antivirus software packages in your enterprise, you can scan, identify, and find these types of malware tools on your hosts and have them removed.

>> You can also see on your outbound firewalls and routers flood-type traffic that should cause your device to raise an alert that a large amount of traffic is going through it or unusual traffic patterns are taking place.

>> Similarly, you can look at the exact same thing on your firewalls and routers or at the processing on the victim machines being flooded with traffic for very high utilization.

Buffer Overflow Attacks

The *buffer overflow attack* is a very common exhaustion of memory on any device in your enterprise that has a buffer (which is pretty much all of them). A *buffer* is an available memory space on a device that allows for incoming traffic to queue so that the system architecture can take it and process it accordingly. This is a very common design that allows your systems (and the hardware everything runs on) to operate correctly.

Figure 6-6 shows the most common use of a buffer overflow attack to overwhelm a network router (externally facing) to overfill the memory so it can't take in any legitimate requests. Legitimate requests would be other incoming connections looking to use resources such as a web page you may host from a server behind a network firewall.

In this attack, I am showing you the most vulnerable aspect of the device to interrupt use based on needed functionality for it to operate correctly. A router must be able to take data and process it to make decisions on where to router traffic. In Figure 6-6, the buffer may be normally at 60% and that's a very busy router. If I as an ethical hacker flood it with traffic to overwhelm it (bring it to 100% utilization), I can then watch as legitimate requests drop which is the normal and intended functionality of the routing device.

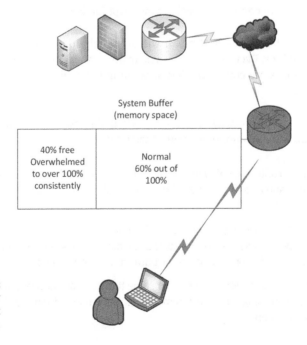

System Buffer
(memory space)

40% free Overwhelmed to over 100% consistently	Normal 60% out of 100%

FIGURE 6-6:
How the buffer overflow attack works.

Although this is hard to identify unless you have a device such as a firewall before your outside router (usually an ISP router that is monitored for this type of attack), you won't know unless you identify disruption of service and trace it back to the router that's being attacked. You could look at the router itself and see packets dropping from being queued.

For example, if this is a Cisco router, you can use the show buffers command to view the output in the queues to see whether packets are flooding in or whether they're being dropped:

```
test-router#show buffers

Buffer elements:
     500 in free list (500 max allowed)
     2370 hits, 72 misses, 0 created

Public buffer pools:
Small buffers, 104 bytes (total 16, permanent 10):
     11 in free list (0 min, 10 max allowed)
     1770 hits, 33 misses, 22 trims, 28 created
     9 failures (0 no memory)
Middle buffers, 600 bytes (total 90, permanent 90):
     89 in free list (10 min, 200 max allowed)
     590 hits, 0 misses, 0 trims, 0 created
     0 failures (0 no memory)
Big buffers, 1524 bytes (total 90, permanent 90):
     90 in free list (5 min, 300 max allowed)
     126 hits, 0 misses, 0 trims, 0 created
     0 failures (0 no memory)
Very Big buffers, 4520 bytes (total 10, permanent 10):
     10 in free list (0 min, 300 max allowed)
     50 hits, 0 misses, 0 trims, 0 created
     0 failures (0 no memory)
Large buffers, 5024 bytes (total 10, permanent 10):
     10 in free list (0 min, 30 max allowed)
     0 hits, 0 misses, 0 trims, 0 created
     0 failures (0 no memory)
Huge buffers, 18024 bytes (total 2, permanent 0):
     0 in free list (0 min, 13 max allowed)
     2 hits, 2 misses, 0 trims, 2 created
     0 failures (0 no memory)
```

Although devices on the market allow for the monitoring of these types of issues and reporting on them from the network hardware vendors, this book only touches on the topic to alert you that, as a pen tester, your toolkit will start to evolve as you look at each and every attack, every vector, and every situation. Here without looking at the device logs and or internals, you may miss what it being attacked and how to prevent it. Similarly, you will want to conduct the same exact ethical attack to ensure that you're not subject to being manipulated by it or at risk.

WARNING

One of the hardest things to understand about how DoS attacks occur is that sometimes the attack cannot be prevented due to how the underlying technology is designed to be used. Back in the original deployment of the TCP/IP suite, for example, the protocols used were designed to be helpful to facilitate interconnectivity, communication, and sharing of resources. As a pen tester your initial response to finding these issues would be to *turn off the service* or remove the risk. There will be times that you must assume the risk and monitor it because there might not be a way to prevent it at the time.

Fragmentation Attacks

A *fragmentation attack* (also known as an *IP fragmentation attack* or *frag attack*) is where IP fragmentation of packets cause a DoS attack. By exploiting the natural design of TCP/IP, a hacker or ethical hacker can send pieces of data to a destination from a source device in hopes that it either causes the DoS, or as a pen tester, shows you that you have a vulnerability to assess.

Frag attacks use the actual protocols as manipulation points instead of the hardware resource available like the buffer.

You can use tools such as Kali's fragroute and fragmentation6 to conduct tests to identify whether you're vulnerable to these types of attacks, as shown in Figure 6-7.

By using fragtest (as shown in Figure 6-8), the Kali toolset allows you to send the malformed packets to hosts to see how they respond. You might need to assess the hosts themselves while conducting these specific tests to identify whether the systems crash, become overwhelmed, or are disrupted.

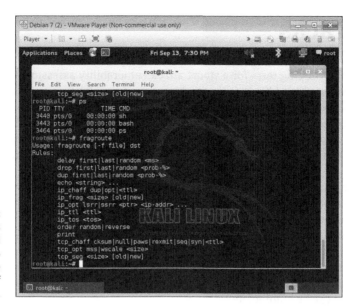

FIGURE 6-7:
Use Kali's fragroute and fragmentation6 to determine your level of vulnerability.

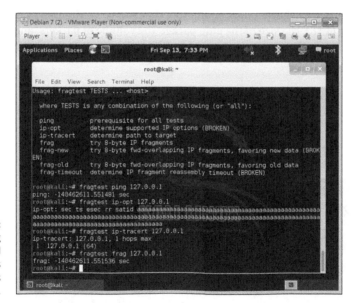

FIGURE 6-8:
Sending malformed packets to hosts with Kali's fragtest.

Smurf Attacks

When running tests for a smurf attack vulnerability assessment don't believe for a minute little blue people will show up and wreak havoc on your systems. Havoc will be created by the actual DDoS attack where ping sweeping is done from spoofed IP addresses to a legitimate host resource in hopes to deny it from functioning correctly. This has nothing to do with the fictional characters and everything to do with real characters trying to create a denial of service attack.

Similar to when a large amount of data causes the DoS that ultimately causes the disruption, with a *smurf attack,* the actual data used to create the overwhelming amount of interrupts of legitimate service comes in the way of the Internet Control Message Protocol (ICMP). This protocol is commonly used in tools such as ping and traceroute (or tracert for Windows). Smurf attacks can be conducted from any device that sends ping sweeps, which is nearly every tool covered in this book (Nessus, Metasploit, Nmap, Kali's tools) but also from any console where ping can be manipulated.

Figure 6-9 shows Linux's ping tool that can be configured to change the time to live (TTL), the size of the ping packet, the volume of packets, and so on that allows for the packets that are changed to create disruption to the network interfaces that will receive it.

REMEMBER

Smurf attacks (and tiny packet and Xmas tree attacks, too) take the technology as it was intended to be used and manipulates it in a way that creates a DoS attack.

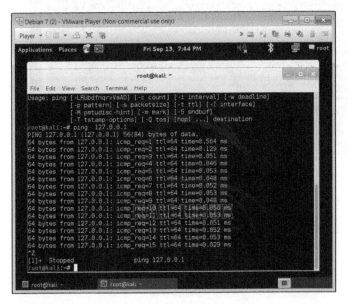

FIGURE 6-9:
Using ping to generate a sweep and smurf attack.

Tiny Packet Attacks

Another easily manipulated technology that can be used for harm is the *tiny packet attack*. Tiny packets are packets that, similar to IP fragmentation attacks, can be further shrunk down to overwhelm the computer buffers receiving them. This DoS attack is part buffer overflow, part fragmentation attack.

This type of attack changes the data packet size, which is normally sized very specifically (as per the standard maximum transmission unit [MTU] size) that routers and other devices expect to see in their buffers. For example, the mid-range (or normal) size of an Ethernet packet is 1,500 bytes. If a hacker starts to send packets that are smaller than 1,500 bytes, the system will have a hard time receiving and processing them, which creates more overhead on the device to process incoming data. In other words, it has to work twice as hard to process that data.

Wireshark is the tool you want to use to identify tiny packets in use on your network. Figure 6-10 shows the Wireshark Packet Lengths menu that shows packets that step outside the 1,500 size norm and the volume in which they appear.

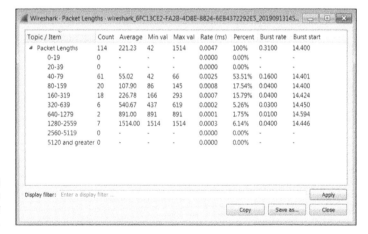

FIGURE 6-10:
Use Wireshark to identify tiny packet attacks.

Xmas Tree Attacks

The *Xmas tree attack* is nothing more than an attack using a *Xmas tree packet,* a packet that is lit up with all options turned on — much like a real Christmas tree set up with lights, ornaments, and tinsel is lit up.

The main reason for this is because the Xmas tree attack is normally used in a stealth mission or reconnaissance for information gathering. It can also be used as a DoS attack: A large number of these packets sent to devices simultaneously can be overwhelming because Xmas tree packets with all options are more process intensive. A large number of them can be twice as intensive and therefore disrupt and overwhelm devices that are performing regular operations.

Chapter **7**

Destroy (Malware)

T he next series of attacks I cover revolves around the destruction of targets or the destruction of the resources provided by targets. The previous chapters in this part cover attacks that are meant to confuse, obfuscate, distract, over- whelm, or disrupt, and maybe even remain completely undetected. But in this chap- ter, I cover the types of attacks meant to simply destroy a company's assets for the purpose of revenge, leverage, gain, or in some cases, for the challenge (or for fun).

Destroy attacks can cost a company a lot of time and money to recover from. You can recover from a destroy attack if you're running a backup program, but your real loss is time. The time it takes to recover the system, data, or resource can be lengthy. If you're running a disaster recovery solution, you could try to move your clients over to another working system, but not all companies have this up and running or have it running in a confident state.

In this chapter I focus on what toolkit tools you need to identify when you're experiencing a destroy type attack, and also whether your systems are vulnerable to that kind of attack.

REMEMBER

Destruction of resources can always be fixed *if* you have an active backup. If the source data/code is destroyed or if some data is lost in transit, and you don't have a backup, it will be lost forever. Make sure to back up data, systems, software, firmware, and access to all of this, and so on. If virtual snapshots of data/systems and VM (virtual machine) hosts are all being taken and performed, you will have a great path to restoring your service very quickly if you need to.

Toolkit Fundamentals

In this section, I show you the tools for conducting a pen test to simulate malware attacks, which are attacks that cause destruction.

Antivirus software and other tools

Tools such as Kali, Nessus (which I discuss further in the following section), Wireshark, and others can be used to scan for vulnerabilities in your systems, so that you can mitigate the risks and the attacks.

Destruction attacks — like all attacks — are hard to identify, so don't limit yourself to your pen test toolkit. You might also want to monitor antivirus (AV) management consoles, firewall logs, routers in the network (to see inbound and outbound traffic patterns), and other tools such as Burp Suite (see Chapter 5) and Metasploit (see Chapter 4).

REMEMBER

Most destruction attacks originate from malicious software (malware). Because of this, the best tool you have in your arsenal will be the antivirus software platforms used in your enterprise. You will find that scanning for vulnerabilities with your toolkit will help, and I explain when this will be relevant, but to identify and remove destructive hacks from your systems, you need to look outside of your toolkit to see the full picture.

Nessus

I discuss Nessus in previous chapters, but the focus in this chapter is using it to scan for vulnerabilities that find:

>> Issues with outdated virus software

>> Malware in the enterprise

>> Other threats that can destroy assets and resources in your network and systems

Figure 7-1 shows different types of scans available by default in Nessus. For example, you might want to run a patch audit to see what systems are vulnerable to being manipulated by exposed code that needs to be fixed by the vendor.

Exposed code refers to software (firmware, operating systems, applications, apps, and so on) that exist that isn't secure when released. Because of this fact, the code needs to be updated, fixed, or even replaced from time to time.

FIGURE 7-1:
Nessus offers various scan types for pen testing destroy attacks.

Normal procedure for most enterprises is to have a patch window or patch cycle (which perhaps opens monthly) to fix all systems impacted by known issues. The patch window can take priority status for issues — identified during pen testing — that point to a known bug or security threat that needs to be patched immediately.

You would run a scan from Nessus that scans a subnet and identifies all hosts that could be vulnerable to known threats. Using Nessus in this fashion (see Figure 7-2) helps you generate a report showing hosts that have malware and or the possibility of being threatened because of known vulnerabilities the tool identifies.

FIGURE 7-2:
Looking for hosts that are vulnerable to known threats.

REMEMBER

A hacker who launches a destroy attack often isn't looking for trade secrets but wants to cause problems and cost you time and money. A company's reputation is usually hit rather hard when something is destroyed, and you have to take a long period of time to repair that reputation. Another reason a hacker launches a destroy attack is to distract you with a sleight of hand. Hackers divert your attention with a logic bomb, for example, and then launch an APT while you're scrambling to handle that. See Chapter 8 for more about subvert attacks.

A pen tester could use these types of ethical hacks and attacks to penetrate systems that are exploitable or vulnerable. When conducting these attacks, you need to make sure that you understand (and report to those you're doing the test for) that you could cause irreversible damage that may only be fixable by restoration or backup.

You could also simulate the attack to probe in a way that you could see whether unpatched systems exploitable by malware are vulnerable.

The attack vector for your hacker can be internal and external. Figure 7-3 shows a typical external vector attack in which the goal would be to inject and destroy a host or database:

>> The database is the target.

>> The goal of the attacker is to launch an attack penetrating the firewall in a web application and injecting a script.

>> The injected script systematically deletes tables from the database host it's connected to in the backend.

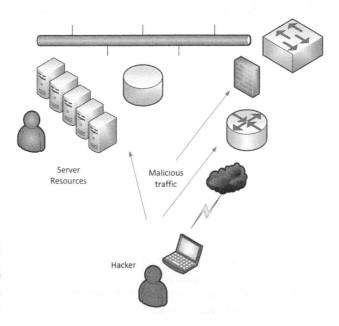

FIGURE 7-3:
A typical external vector attack with the goal of destroying a database.

This example shows a very simple design in which the attacker destroys assets using a script that could have been delivered in a variety of ways:

>> From a Trojan horse application inserted on a host inside the network.

>> Sent in an email with an attached virus (malware) that spreads perhaps like a worm that caused attacks against the database that could corrupt it.

>> Someone walking into the data center, getting on a console, and deleting files.

>> Conducted remotely from a trusted (but potentially disgruntled) user from the safety of their home over VPN.

TIP

By looking at NAC (network access control) software from vendors such as Forescout, you will have a better chance at finding, exposing, and protecting against destroy-style attacks. NAC denies (and quarantines) systems that come online in your network with any malware present or not meeting the expectations of the policies set forth by the administrators. They are placed on a protected network segment and addressed (possibly fixed or repaired) prior to being allowed to participate on the network.

Malware

Malware (or *malicious software*) is the most common form of vulnerability faced by almost every single organization that uses technology today. This is a global issue and it doesn't discriminate in any way. If you're connected to a network and use its resources, it's likely you have at one time in your life come across some form of malware — be it viruses, worms, or Trojan horses.

Types of malware include but are not limited to:

>> **Virus:** A simple program created to replicate itself to other computers, systems, and programs when it's executed. The most common theme with a virus is that it needs to be executed to be harmful, so it's usually followed by some form of trickery to get someone to execute it. This trickery can be in the form of phishing, social engineering, click baiting, and so on.

>> **Worm:** A worm is similar to a virus and a bad form of malware in that it is self-replicating. The worm uses holes in your security that it can piggyback on to replicate.

>> **Trojan horse:** In ancient Greek mythology, the Trojan horse was used to trick those who thought it to be a gift to accept it and bring it into their fortified protected area (through their gates), unknowing that within it was a great many soldiers ready to do battle. This is why this piece of malware is called a Trojan horse. It misleads you into thinking it is something you want or need, but in the background contains a piece of malware causes you harm.

A Trojan horse (sometimes just simply referred to as a Trojan) is devastating to those who install it because it essentially can spy on you (capture your passwords/credentials), activate and use your machine (to launch attacks), and other things, too, such as leave a backdoor open to your enterprise systems from the host it has occupied.

>> **Spyware:** Spyware does exactly what it says; it spies on you and your activities while lying dormant on your system. It can collect information and send it to those who might find value in the collected data sent by the malware.

>> **Zero day:** A zero day is simply a piece of code that has an exploit that has yet to be identified. It's ripe for the picking by hackers if they find it before you do. It's one of the hardest attacks to prevent. Zero days can come from failed coding by a vendor or a purposeful code exploit or malware. Either way — the zero day event is because no one knows about it yet.

>> **Logic bomb:** The logic bomb is malware code set to activate based on a set of criteria taking place. For example, as the payload, a bomb could be to delete a bunch of files on your local computer at a certain time, a certain key stroke, or a certain click, which would be the logic that activates it.

>> **Ransomware:** Covered in more detail in the next section, this type of malware happens to be one of the most devastating. It feels worse than the others because you're left to interact with the hacker — who has caused you this problem and who is demanding a ransom for the release of your property.

Ransomware is a destroy attack with a timer. If you fail to pay the ransom, the encrypted data is held hostage forever and you can't use it thus leaving it in a devastated state. Anyone who doesn't have reliable and timely backups is left helpless.

Ransomware

Ransomware is its own brand of evil. Those who create it and distribute it are some of the worst of the bunch because this is a script kiddie paradise. The elite hackers who created the tool in the first place have left a tool like WannaCry (one of the most common ransomware attacks) to those who can use it to extort good people out of money. There are others, like Petya. Regardless of how many variants exist, they all do the same basic function: Encrypt your data so you're unable to use it, and then make you pay a large amount of money to decrypt it.

Figure 7-4 shows an example of WannaCry and how the attack is conducted. The end user in your organization could have visited a website with the tool on it and downloaded it thinking it was something they needed. They get a nasty surprise when they find out what they actually downloaded: an encryption tool on their system that can conduct an attack when activated.

FIGURE 7-4:
An example of a ransomware attack.

REMEMBER

When considering destroy type attacks and your role as a pen tester, the ultimate goal is to identify gaps in your security before any malware lands on your systems and causes you and your company problems.

The question to ask yourself is: How do I test systems and infrastructure to make sure I am secure against malware attacks?

The answer is: Conduct assessments with pen test tools and other tools appropriate to the company's enterprise management and monitoring system, identify if any issues exist, determine where those issues could cause problems, and finally mitigate the risk before the hacks and attacks take place in the first place.

This is similar to what you would do to protect against any type of attack, but in the case of malware, I recommend first putting on the security analyst hat. You must make sure your company has a great enterprise management and monitoring tool such as antivirus (AV) software deployed across the enterprise to protect all endpoints from attack. Endpoints can be any device such as a laptop, computer, mobile device, or tablet.

Figure 7-5 shows an example of the most commonly used tool to prevent malware attacks, which is endpoint protection through an AV tool. Although this is the most common and helpful, it doesn't completely solve the problem.

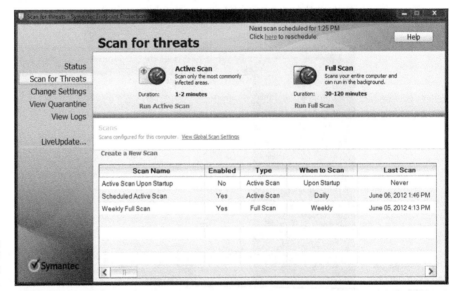

FIGURE 7-5:
An example of AV endpoint protection.

Additionally, you must do the following:

>> **Ensure the AV tool is managed and maintained.** This means that the tool itself is updated with all the latest scanning information required to stay on top of the latest threats.

>> **Secure the endpoints.** Every endpoint in your enterprise that runs some form of software (or firmware) is susceptible to malware. Pen testing can come to the rescue, of course, by helping you to identify all the endpoints and which are vulnerable.

By running the tools I cover in this chapter (and in Chapter 8, where I cover subvert attacks, another attack against AV), you'll notice that simple assessments identify many of your systems as susceptible to attack. Why? Because hackers work night and day to uncover holes in the software itself and write code attacks to expose the holes they find. The vendors then write code (hotfixes, service packs, and patches) for you to download and install on the machine to protect it. Running a pen test will tell you that 15 percent of your workstations aren't running the latest patches. You can then download and install them to protect your systems.

The pen tester's job is never done, and you must remain proactive with your scans to identify threats before they occur.

Running pen tests, using good AV software, finding risks and fixing them all provides a good level of protection applied to your enterprise. But you can't consider this to be how you fully protect against malware. You must remain diligent in your testing because there is a constant effort underway to undermine security to get this bad code through your door. Social engineering is the best way for hackers to get in and get someone to click something and download it. You can pen test this by educating your end users. If an educated end user knows not to click something, then they can avoid activating malware. Does it stop all of it? No, but it will limit attacks significantly.

Other Types of Destroy Attacks

Other destroy attacks aren't very fancy but just as brutal as the code-based ones. Although they may not have a fancy name, many manual attacks can destroy assets all the same. In these attacks, the vectors are just as difficult to determine as the malware-based ones (which can come from anywhere — email, weblink, and so on). Attacks that thwart physical access, the vector is as simple as a person leaving their computer open, which means someone else can sit down and go to work.

The damage an attacker can do would essentially be sabotage, which can take various forms, to cause a destroy-based attack:

>> Mass deletion of files

>> The insertion of a virus or malware

>> The intentional corruption of data

» The insertion of a payload

» The changing of settings or injecting errors

» An injection overload to corrupt

Hackers look for these attacks because they are easy, require far less time and resources, and are the ones that leave little to no trail other than what security cameras might pick up.

REMEMBER

Consider the physical security, too: access control from cameras, card swipes, biometrics, and other forms of security (security guards) can help you prevent these types of attacks. Remember, defense in depth extends to the physical realm, so don't overlook it.

Chapter **8**

Subvert (Controls Bypass)

The definition of *subvert* is to undermine and get within control. In the realm of IT security, this means you get within and beyond controls or control points that are meant to secure access. Subvert attacks bring their own intense brand of nastiness to the security equation.

Advanced persistent threats (APTs) are the holy grail of hacker attacks where an attacker can infiltrate, gain what they need, and then move to exfiltration undetected with the goods. There are other attacks that are less advanced such as bypassing controls such as an access list without being caught or logging into a system undetected to access data. Some malware can also be introduced to elevate privileges of accounts that can then be used to bypass other security controls.

In this chapter, I discuss these and other forms of subvert attacks.

Toolkit Fundamentals

In this section, I show you the tools for conducting a pen test to simulate subvert attacks, which are attacks that get past security controls. Tools such as Kali, Nmap (which I discuss further in an upcoming section), Wireshark, and others can be used to scan for vulnerabilities in your systems. As with so many attacks, subvert attacks can be difficult to track. To mitigate the risks and the attacks, I recommend going outside your pen test toolkit.

Antivirus software and other tools

Many subvert attacks originate from malware. Because of this, the best tool you have in your arsenal is antivirus software platforms used in your enterprise. I focus the final section of this chapter on how attackers thwart your security by getting around your AV tool.

TIP

Other tools in your toolkit include (but aren't limited to) Kali, Nmap, Wireshark, AV management consoles, router and firewall logs, and others. For subvert attacks the focus will be on probing and mapping to find an entry point. Once an entry point is found, there needs to be movement within the network and then finding a way to stay hidden.

TIP

To learn more about subvert attacks, I recommend researching the Open Web Application Security Project (OWASP; www.owasp.org), which I discuss in Chapter 16.

Nmap

There is no better tool used to probe, map, and identify holes and ways through them than Nmap. Nessus, Metasploit, and even Kali offer many tools to perform this function, but Nmap itself is the go-to for this type of attack.

REMEMBER

Kali has Nmap and several other mapping tools within its toolset. Open Kali and navigate to the Information Gathering menu (see Figure 8-1) to access a series of categories you can drill further into for a tool to help you perform subvert and stealth-based attacks.

Using Nmap to simulate subvert attacks

Here are some reasons why Nmap helps to simulate subvert attacks:

>> **Nmap is customizable and can be script driven.** You can set up scripts to execute based on the programming you create to launch attacks.

>> **Nmap does exactly what is needed to scan, probe, map and identify weaknesses especially needed for a subvert attack.**

>> **You can conduct varying levels of attacks from low to high intensity.** This allows for a very quick pen test scan of your weaknesses, all the way to very involved highly intense and robust scanning that can help to really show you over time what problems exist.

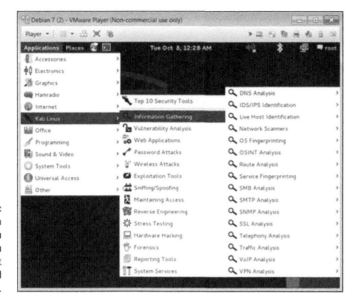

FIGURE 8-1:
Kali's Information
Gathering menu
can help you
perform subvert
and stealth-based
attacks.

WARNING

Remember that Nmap is a scanning tool and will probe and test your systems. If you're using this on a production network, it could create issues or set off alarms. Make sure you have permission to launch this tool prior to doing so.

Putting Nmap to work

As shown in Figure 8-2, I have launched an attack against a router/routing device scan. My goal is to identify all devices on a subnet by scanning hosts and trying to identify them and map them. This also allows me to build a list of vulnerabilities that I may be able to exploit.

Running a scan against a host may be captured by security devices, which will show the IP address of origination (your IP address). Many times, these attacks are leveraged from spoofed addresses or hosts that have been hijacked and owned by the hacker — usually through malware such as a Trojan horse — so they aren't caught.

In this example, I am choosing an intense scan, which generates the most output for my report, because:

» I am not on a production network.

» I am limiting my scan to one host at a time as I am aware of the network topology.

FIGURE 8-2:
Using Nmap to
launch an attack
against a router/
routing device
scan.

As shown in Figure 8-3, this intense scan is mapping the vulnerabilities through a series of test scans looking for open ports and other penetration points. The main penetration test I am launching right at this point is a SYN Stealth Scan, which is designed to use SYN packets at a host or hosts in hopes of receiving an acknowledgment from a host in the form of an ACK packet.

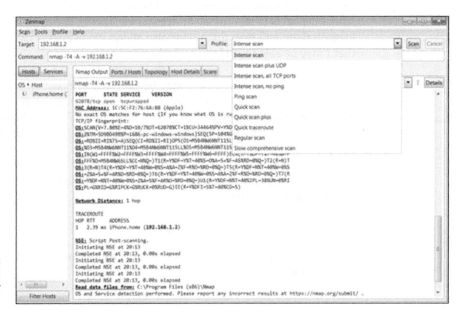

FIGURE 8-3:
Conducting a SYN
scan to identify
open ports.

HOW TCP/IP WORKS

TECHNICAL STUFF

The way that TCP/IP is used as protocols to create bi-directional communication between hosts is by establishing a communication channel through a series of packet transfers known as a handshake. Much like when meeting someone new and introducing yourself and then they do the same, having a common goal of embrace such as a handshake creates a bond. In TCP/IP, this handshake does the exact same things except it creates a channel as a bond. To do this, the source host will send packets out SYN, then the destination sends back a SYN/ACK and then the source provides the three-way handshake final communication of an ACK. Once this happens, a connection is established and maintained between the devices until terminated. This may be seen as a reset packet that is known as RST.

TIP

You can run this test without knowledge of TCP/IP and gain the same information, but knowing how the technology works helps. See the nearby sidebar for more about TCP/IP.

Figure 8-4 shows the SYN Stealth Scan identifying a host and a possible host that responded, which is the source of my next attack. Other identifiable information was found (see Figure 8-5), which includes the MAC address of the device being scanned and distance by network hop.

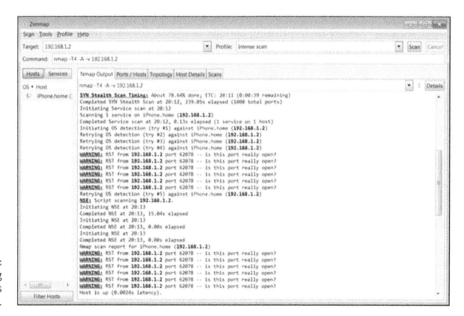

FIGURE 8-4:
Identifying possible hosts and ports.

FIGURE 8-5:
Learning the MAC
address of the
scanned device
and distance by
network hop.

You can do so much more with Nmap, and it's a must for this next series of subvert attacks I cover.

REMEMBER

Throughout the rest of this chapter, I remain focused on using Nmap to perform
a bypass from a spoofed address to launch an APT. However, continue to drill
down in a safe lab environment into some of these other tool offerings, such as the
many fingerprinting options available, the SMB mapping tool (which is helpful to
identify holes in Microsoft networks), and others.

ETHICALLY CONDUCTING SUBVERT ATTACKS

I want to get into some of the cyberwarfare/cybercrime details you may need to know
to better position yourself to conduct these ethical hacks. The history revolving around
subvert attacks traces back decades and has been a part of war (and now cyberwar) for
many years.

Stealth operations (black ops) have been a big part of threat actors of groups such as
nation state or state sponsored groups looking to find secrets or other usable intelligence data to gain advantage. Companies do this as well to gain intellectual property so
they too can gain financial leverage.

By gaining unauthorized access and remaining inside to exfiltrate data for an extended
period of time you have officially conducted an APT. It all starts with identification and
infiltration and this is where all subvert attacks ultimately originate from.

Attack Vectors

To help explain attack vectors, Figure 8-6 shows that regardless of whether an attack originates from inside or outside your protected network, the concepts are the same. I am going to conduct a pen test to first see if I can probe your network. I may do this from a spoofed address or I may launch an attack from a Trojan installed on a machine that a victim may not be aware of.

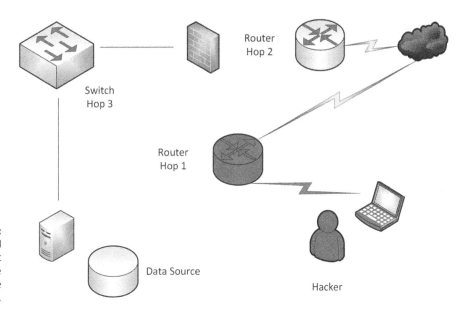

FIGURE 8-6:
Internal and external subvert attacks operate under the same concepts.

In this attack vector, the hacker (in this case, me) is looking to gain access and do so undetected. By infiltrating the network step by step (or hop by hop), I can begin sneaking my way inside to collect information from valuable data sources. Here's how I did it:

1. **The first hop will be through a router I scanned with Nmap and found that it was vulnerable due to a weak password.**

   By conducting a password crack, I am inside the first hop and ready to attempt to gain access to the next hop. Once in this router, I am able to conduct a series of next steps to find more information: I can look at the routing table, the MAC address table, ARP cache, and other non-proprietary features to learn where to go next.

   I can look at the router's configuration file and see how it is configured. For example, if I see that there is a port connected to another network with an IP address and subnet mask associated for only four valid hosts to include the network and broadcast identifiers, I can assume that if the one configured IP address is 10.1.1.2, perhaps the next one across the wide area network (WAN) link may be 10.1.1.3. I can quickly ping or attempt to telnet to the next hop to see.

Proprietary systems such as Cisco brand routers also use other protocols and services such as CDP (Cisco Discovery Protocol), which allows for the building of a database of neighbors that can be accessed by running the show CDP neighbors command as another example on how to get information on adjacent hosts.

2. **I can attempt to access router hop 2 and do the same procedure as hop 1.**

3. **I then attempt to get to hop 3, which is a switch that also accepts telnet as an option.**

I also list a firewall host between the router and the switch, but this may signify an access control list (ACL) that disallows traffic or attempts and may not be an actual separate firewall device.

If the router or any other device is misconfigured and allows connections through, I am able to get to the third hop.

Once I am able to maintain a connection in the third hop, I may be able to run a ping sweep from the switch device or look at the MAC table to see what may be connected. Inside I find a Linux host that I find interesting because it too accepts connections from telnet and allows me to quickly password crack and gain access to the system.

Here I can then look through the system and see whether it hosts any internal data I can use, or I can remain dormant to see whether there are other secrets elsewhere at another time.

Although this is a simplified explanation of a pen attack with a lot of misconfigurations and protocols that should be disabled and more secure versions used (such as SSH instead of telnet), it does not mean that this attack is unachievable. Believe it or not, this exact hack is still being conducted today.

What it should teach you as a pen tester is that the attack vector and path taken would be the same no matter what types of attacks were used or attempted. If a piece of malware was inside your network and a hacker can control the host it is attached to, they would conduct this exact series of attacks.

Phishing

One of the main options for a hacker is to gain access to a host computer through *phishing*, which is a technical version of social engineering. You are using an email hoax or information to entice someone to do something (such as click a link), which can lead to click bait or clickjacking attacks that install software on your machine to gain access to it. That machine then becomes part of the hacker toolkit to gain access to your systems.

As a pen tester, you need to attempt this same attack on your internal users to see whether they are smart or trained well enough to know to not click a phishing attempt. If they're presented with something that looks fishy (pun intended), do the users know what they can do to thwart what might be a possible attack?

The clickjacking attack is very similar. The hacker tricks a victim to click something they perceive to be something else. The victim clicks, for example, a link they think is legitimate, and the hacker can gain access or control that system.

It's kind of like a standard carjacking but with click bait instead. An attacker is going to trick you into giving something up by making you provide it through trickery.

How this relates to subvert attacks and stealth ops is that the victim becomes part of the attacker's hack. When victims allow themselves to be fooled, they become part of the path or vector of the attack the hacker is launching. You should be comfortable with constructing a fake link that redirects to another page or site (informing the user they have been fooled) from a real-looking address and provide materials for them to review on how to identify these types of attacks in an educational way.

Spoofing

Spoofing is the way an attacker disguises their identity and remains hidden. If I launch an attack from Nmap and need to hide my identity, I can either do it from a hacked source or directly from the tool itself.

As an example, when you launch Nmap, you can use the –S option, which spoofs your source address into whatever address you would like to choose. Other ways to spoof are pretty well documented online based on the tools you choose, but because Nmap is the focus here, attempt to add the –S `<ip_address>` information and use Wireshark on the receiving host to see the spoof attack. To conduct a spoofing attack, such as Man in The Middle (MiTM) or other subvert attacks, see Chapter 5.

Another example of spoofing would be when a hacker makes an email look legitimate to the recipient. But it's easily seen as a spoof through the email header, where the fake address is usually listed. This kind of spoof happens to people all the time — they get an email from their email provider (or so they think) saying that their account has been compromised and they need to log into their account to fix it. When they do, they give the attacker their username and password.

Malware

In this section, I shine a light on the inner workings of how an attacker uses AV software and malware to get into your system. It should be no wonder (or mistake) that the best way to get in undetected is through malware. The original vector I describe earlier in this chapter, in the "Attack Vectors" section, going hop from hop leaves a huge footprint in the sand. You can get caught at any point in that path.

As you move from system to system you may be caught by other tools and logs. As well, you need to clean and sanitize hop from hop to eliminate being seen, which sometimes means wiping logs that can identify you. It all depends on how much security an enterprise uses and has deployed. For any company with much to lose (and much to gain for a hacker), it seems likely that they will have much of this security gear deployed.

Using malware to find a way in

Malware is one of the best ways in, so using this to your advantage can reap many rewards. Obviously by running tools such as Nessus and other vulnerability assessors, you will find what systems are unpatched, are vulnerable, and have more holes than Swiss cheese. This doesn't mean that it covers all vectors. Just because you patch a system doesn't mean it's safe from attack.

If a system gets malware on it that disables the protection from a host level as shown in Figure 8-7, you may not see it until it's too late. For example, this version of Symantec Endpoint Protection (SEP) has been disabled, causing it to allow malware to pass due. It requires updates due to a long disable period. If you don't see it on the host system or whoever is managing it didn't fix it, malware could have slipped by. You can also cause it to fail manually by locally accessing the host.

In Figure 8-8, the only way to re-enable and fix your AV is by either having it done remotely at the management console or if you fix it yourself locally at the local workstation.

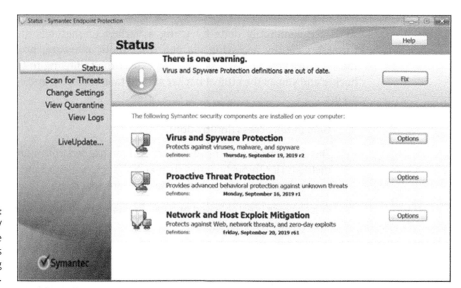

FIGURE 8-7:
Host-based AV software indicates there's an issue requiring attention.

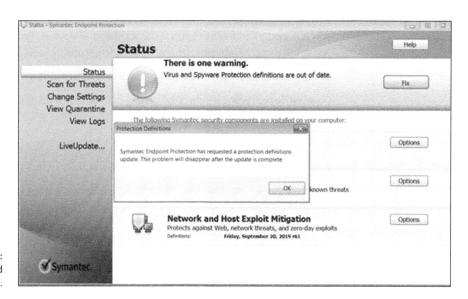

FIGURE 8-8:
Updating and fixing your AV.

Bypassing AV software

AV bypass is common and one way to get through your host-based defenses. Local firewalls are passed in the same fashion. Once this happens, malware, viruses, worms, Trojan horses, backdoor/rootkits and other nasty pieces of code will enter and allow for further attacks remotely. The attacks can happen locally, too; raised privileges or escalated privileges on the host machine allows more access than the user may have had previously.

APTs are commonly done by using a variety of methods such as infiltration through code, by accessing via pen tests tools, malware, programs, and other means. Once you gain access, you can expect the following to take place from the hacker and you as the ethical hacker should take each step and ensure that you are secure:

1. **Gain initial access (infiltration).**

   This is the first step in the APT attack and can happen from many of the methods I list throughout this chapter. You should re-enact them to ensure your systems are safe and your end users are educated.

2. **Once access is established and can be maintained, work to protect that access and keep it a secret.**

   This is done through stealth ops and by maintaining those operations by any means possible.

3. **Now that access is secure and secret, start attempting to move around, gaining more access, and identifying data or targets to access.**

   This is done by continuing to run tests, access other devices, find targets, penetrate them, all while remaining secret and secure.

4. **Complete the APT by exfiltration of data and information.**

   Do so while remaining inside or by getting out with the data and without getting caught.

3

Diving In: Preparations and Testing

Chapter **9**

Preparing for the Pen Test

B ecoming familiar with types of attacks and a pen tester's tools are necessary early steps to using those tools to protect a company's assets against hackers and their nefarious intentions. Before you dive into the testing, assessing, and preventing, however, there are certain preparatory tasks to take care of.

In addition to knowing what attack type you're exploring and what tools you need to use to do that, you must understand your role, which systems you're testing (or not), and what the stakeholder's goals and expectations are. I cover all of that in this chapter and more, including what to do if you have to end a test before it even gets started.

Handling the Preliminary Logistics

Before you get to the part where you will do any pen testing, you must work out certain logistical details, including getting permission to do the tests. This section highlights and explains those logistics.

Holding an initial meeting

You'll want to have a meeting to discuss roles, responsibilities, and expectations. This brings together all involved parties, who are assisting with the scan, mitigating any risks that may be found, or simply providing the necessary permission to have the work done.

In this section, I focus on what will happen in the initial meeting with the stakeholders — roles established, expectations discussed, the scope defined. Note that a series of meetings will be necessary, however, as you begin other preparations, which involves gathering requirements. The stakeholders might decide to set up a weekly meeting, or have them even twice a week, for the life of the project.

Understanding everyone's role

You must understand what role you're playing in the scenario in front of you. For example, if you're working for a large company as part of their in-house security team, conducting a pen test will be slightly different than if you're hired as an outside consultant who will assess and pen test for the client. You'll do everything the same, but the role you play may be slightly different.

Note that, as a pen tester, your role is first and foremost to conduct penetration tests to find weaknesses in an organization's security plan. You might or might not be expected to make recommendations on your findings and then implement those recommendations to secure the identified weaknesses. That all might be someone else's responsibility, too, making it so important to hash out these issues ahead of time.

As a pen tester (especially one who is a consultant), you may want to suggest a clear identification of roles and responsibilities. Figure 9-1 shows a generic RACI (Responsible, Accountable, Consulted, and Informed) chart that you can customize however you see fit. This chart is used to list who is part of the project, who's responsible for what, who's accountable for specific tasks, and so on.

This chart is a good way to verify the scope and set boundaries, as well as document the set of deliverables and who will perform them and keep concerned parties involved to the necessary level (consulted, informed).

Setting expectations

If the expectation is that you will conduct a pen test to test the security of the enterprise, you have been given a very wide and non-specific task to follow. You may need to cast a wide net to get a good catch.

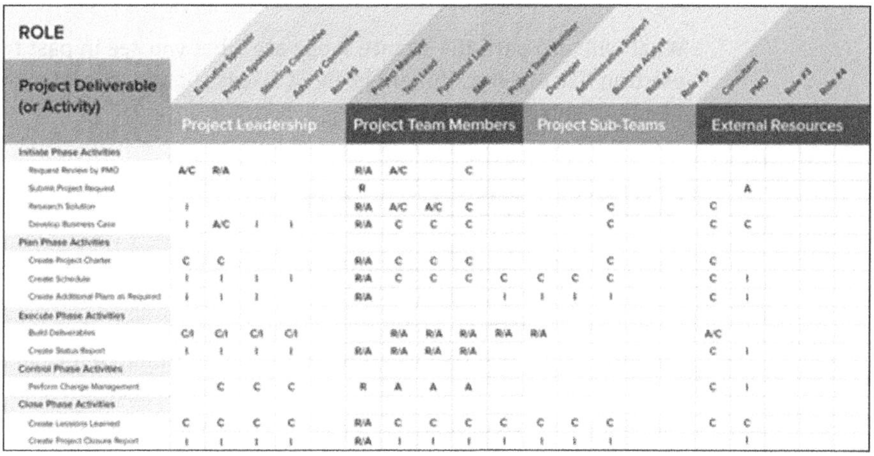

FIGURE 9-1:
Use a RACI chart to identify roles and responsibilities.

On the other hand, you might be given a very specific task such as ensuring the company's trade secrets are safe from prying eyes — internally and externally. You now have a more specific goal to accomplish.

Setting scope

Clarifying what exactly your task will be is determining the *scope* of your work. Whoever is asking for your services should detail the scope up front. The scope discussion should absolutely be part of your meetings with stakeholders because they're setting the expectations and goals. Topics to discuss include

>> Whether this is an in-house pen test or a consultant pen test.

>> Whether this is a one-off task or part of a program.

>> If part of a program, how retesting will be handled.

BUILDING A TEST PLAN BASED ON GOALS

Going with these two examples, if the first one is given as task, you may want to start with vulnerability scans, and mapping scans to identify threats, then if you find weaknesses, move into each to test whether you can exploit them. All your reports may produce these artifacts so that they can be reviewed later to identify problem areas that you may want to retest (which I will cover in Chapter 12). If the other example is used where a more specific deliverable is given and you can focus your attention in that one area, you will be able to dig right into a potential problem spot and penetration test until you do or do not find exploits.

What will also partially dictate scope are what you see in past test results and the existing risk register, if there is one. I discuss both in the later section, "Gathering Requirements."

Gaining permission

Being a great pen tester requires you to make great assessments about the pen testing you're conducting. You are an ethical hacker conducting an active penetration on an enterprise network with permission. This means you will have to ask for permission, and that might require going through a formal process.

Gaining permission to conduct a pen test is a multifaceted process. Many aspects fall under the umbrella of what you should discuss early on:

>> It depends on the size of the company and those who are tasking you to accomplish it. Who ultimately gives permission might not be anyone you're dealing with directly but who's higher up the chain of command.

>> There also needs to be specific guidelines on next steps and what you have the access and rights to do.

For example, you may find a weakness outside the boundaries you were given and think it's a threat. The right thing to do is to escalate it to those who need to know immediately and seek further guidance, not probe and try to exploit it.

>> Gaining permission should be part of the first series of meetings that take place once the roles have been assigned and the tasks have been agreed upon and approved.

>> You may want to have a test done in covert fashion to really test those who might be involved in securing systems. You may need to obtain separate permission to do this.

>> You may also corrupt data (so you need a backup), or you may cause another problem that needs to be addressed. These are also issues to address during the permission discussion.

>> You will have a strategy for how you'll approach and conduct the pen test. Share this strategy with the stakeholders, so they understand your method and everyone knows what you're doing, and they can confidently provide you the permission to do your job.

Following change control

You will likely need to do a change control to document the fact that a change (scanning, testing, and attempting of changes on your network and systems) will be taking place.

Change control is necessary to document what is happening but also to log the time, date, and other useful information needed if an incident arises from the scan itself and support teams need to mobilize to assist. A critical prep item should be a contingency plan if something goes wrong. See "Having a Backout Plan," later in this chapter, for more about contingency plans.

In my experience, I have seen older systems and interfaces fail due to excessive scanning that caused a technical failure to occur. I have also seen triggers, thresholds, and alerts set that starts to shut down things when an attack may be present and cause a production outage. Also, your operations teams (who may not be on the RACI or know about the scans) may start to see suspicious activity and think they are under attack and start to respond to a false positive.

All these scenarios and more can be solved with a change ticket and/or change control. In the cases where you may not be able to follow this process (smaller companies might not have a process), you may want to consider an alternative so that you can track the work being done and avoid issues.

Keeping backups

Make sure you not only have backup of data, but backup of systems, software, firmware, access to all of this, and so on. If virtual, snapshots of data/systems VMs hosts and other pertinent data suffice.

Having documentation

Larger companies might automatically have everything in writing. If not, ask to have documentation in place that authorizes your scan (and all your activities) and any steps needed to restore data, recover from disaster, and so on.

Gathering Requirements

Gathering requirements is based on the scope of what needs to be done, but at the same time, the requirements you gather might indicate what needs to be done — and that could be different from what you or stakeholders expected. For example, the scenarios provided in this chapter can still serve to show you differences in the requirement gathering process. If I am going to do a wide assessment versus a deep and specific assessment, the requirements for each might be different. In this example, the wide assessment may require a set of tools and specific access to the network both internally and externally. In another scenario, you may only need to scan internally and start your pen test from a wireless access point.

REMEMBER

This is why it is crucial to assess past results and the risk register — it helps you define the scope. You need that to refine the actual tools, strategy, vectors, and strategies to accomplish a good pen test. As you refine your strategy, you will provide status updates at the regular stakeholder meetings I discuss earlier in this chapter. Keeping everyone apprised will ensure no one (including you) gets a nasty surprise.

Reviewing past test results

The next part of assessment and prep work is in looking at what has already been done before you start to conduct your pen test. The reason you do this is because the more you know, the better equipped you'll be. This is especially important if you're conducting a pen test for a company for the first time. Find out what you can from previous assessments (and check the risk register, which I cover next) to discover if you need to do an immediate retest and see if you still have open vulnerabilities based on previous assessments.

If you've done pen tests for this company before, you may have (and I really hope you do!) saved reports or logs in assessment tools already available to review as shown in Figure 9-2. Part of testing is to make sure you're documenting the experience so that you can either mitigate the risks or document them and monitor them if you can't repair them. Having that documentation for future reference is invaluable.

TIP

If and when possible, discuss with other IT security team members who have conducted previous assessments. Ask them for any artifacts from past results and scans that they can share. Remember, use the RACI chart, so you know who you are authorized to talk to and what you are allowed to divulge.

Consulting the risk register

The risk register is where all the vulnerabilities you find and need to mitigate wind up. If previous pen tests have already been conducted, there should already be a risk register with entries you can review. Figure 9-3 shows risk register metrics you can consult to determine whether there are areas in which you may want to tailor your current scans, tests, and assessments.

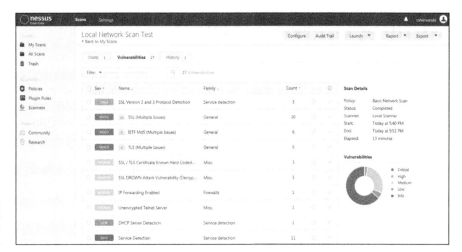

FIGURE 9-2:
Consult past
results to help
with future tests.

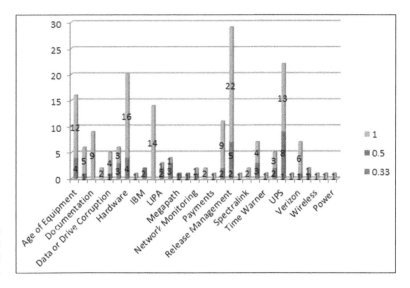

FIGURE 9-3:
Reviewing threats
on the risk
register.

For example, you may find that a large number of vulnerabilities in a Release Management category. You may find that as updates are sent to the enterprise, it causes more problems than can be fixed, solved, or mitigated. In this case, you might decide to run pen tests that test the integrity of your desktop systems, applications, and other programs to make sure no known vulnerabilities still exist (or new ones have cropped up) in this focus area.

Coming Up with a Plan

After you have consulted prior test results and the risk register, you're getting closer to being ready to conduct a pen test. What you've assessed so far in this chapter, as an example, has shown the need to do a wide scan first and then drill down to specific areas that may present threats. Recovering any data of value in an APT type format is desired as an expected outcome.

Figure 9-4 shows the attack vector. Broken into steps, it looks like this:

1. An internal user comes in via wireless.

2. The user attempts to find access to a database with valuable information and remain undetected.

3. The user continues to access data until exfiltrating undetected with the company data.

With this information in hand, you can select tools you believe may be helpful in getting this pen test accomplished, deciding the best vectors to take, and determining how you could go about doing this exact test in Chapter 10.

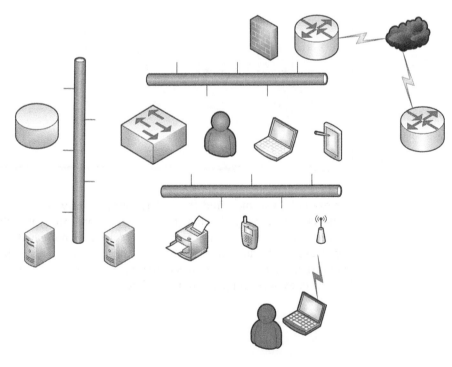

FIGURE 9-4:
Reviewing attack
vectors to devise
a test plan.

Selecting a project or scan type

When preparing for a pen test, one of the first things you need to pre-plan is the tool selection because once you know what tools you need, you know what options are available within the tools.

REMEMBER

This may seem like common sense and it is; however, there are many variables based on the scan type, what the stakeholders are asking for, if you're just running a quarterly, monthly, or annual scan or possibly just running a test of your tools for accuracy or practice. Because of these variables, consider what tool you need to use and then what vectors you are accessing. For example, you need different tools to access a wired network versus a wireless network.

Next to consider are the types of scans you may do to gain information. Because you need to be connected to a wireless network to conduct the test, consider wireless enabled tools such as Wireshark and its wireless functions. Other scan types you may want to consider revolve around network mapping (Nmap) and a basic network scan with Nessus (see Figure 9-5) and others to gain the info you need to conduct an APT.

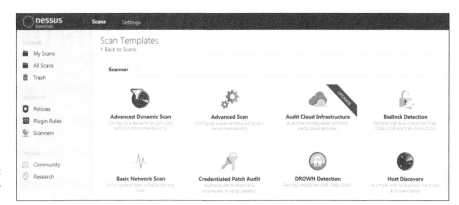

FIGURE 9-5:
Reviewing Nessus
scan templates.

Selecting the tool(s)

In this section you select your tools. In general, you use the most common of tools (including Nessus, Nmap, Kali, Wireshark) and other system and operating system tools to help you conduct an APT.

Before getting started with the pen test, you also need to get your toolkits ready for the task. For example, if you know that you may want to see whether you can access FTP servers, you can tailor a set of FTP filters that can pull the specific info needed immediately. Based on what data you're able to gather, you may need to search for usernames and passwords sent that can be used in your APT. Figure 9-6 shows Wireshark's filter option that can be used quickly to get to the data you need.

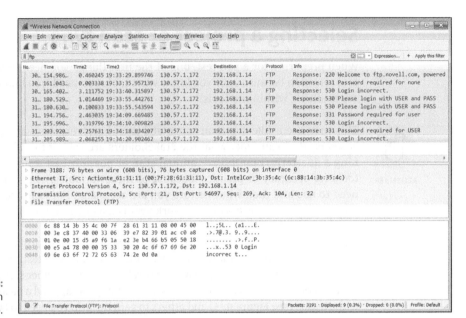

FIGURE 9-6:
Tuning tools with filters for prep.

REMEMBER

CONSIDERATIONS BEFORE PEN TESTING

Before you begin the actual pen test, take a deep breath and consider the plan you have established. Consider the following tips so that you can not only be successful, but not have mishaps that could tarnish your reputation or that of the clients.

- **Staying focused is important.** As a pen tester, you're probably by nature curious. You push the limits and find holes that you can drive through to get to your goal. This is very different than an actual organizational-sponsored penetration test that you have permission for. There may be guidelines that you need to follow.

- **Staying on target is important.** You have a plan; stick to it. You can consider options and alternatives, but you need to document them as opportunities in your logs.

For example, I personally try to hack into a router by exploiting a weak password. The next step is to see what my next hop is. I look at the routing table and find a series of routes in a Cisco router using the show ip route command. I may find a route I wasn't looking to and probe it to see what the router tells me.

```
RouterA# show ip route 130.115.0.0
Routing entry for 130.115.0.0 (mask 255.255.0.0)
    Known via "igrp 100", distance 100, metric 10989
    Tag 0
```

```
    Redistributing via igrp 100
    Last update from 130.109.20.10 on ETH0, 0:00:58 ago
```

At this point I may be interested in learning more about the routing infrastructure and how it's mapped, what else the router may tell me, and so on. However, I have enough information right now to get to where I need to go for my mission. Staying on target helped me not lose focus. I don't need to know much more about this router; however, I may identify something I want to bring up that could be problematic. For example, the router I logged into reported the code version of the operations system that I know have bugs associated with it. So, I enter that into the log.

From the viewpoint of vulnerability scanning, imagine you get permission to scan and identify hosts on a particular network that you requested permission to do, alerted your customers/clients, and submitted change management documentation that may have turned off alerts in those parts of the network. If you decide to scan outside of this block, you may potentially create chaos, so you have to be specific and, in some cases, precise with your approach.

If you do get permission to do otherwise, then you're free to conduct any level of test you are sanctioned for.

Having a Backout Plan

Before you begin, you should already know how you will terminate when you need to. If a pen test is causing an impact, you should consider dealing with the impact and stopping the pen test. If you have an impact based on a tool being run, stop the tool or pause it so you don't lose your place.

For example, some scan tools are pausable so you can start the scan again from where you left off and not duplicate your efforts. Regardless, you're one of the good guys so if you're seeing an impact (or an impact is brought to your attention), shut down your test and reassess where you are and what is happening so you can resume later. If you break something, get it fixed. If you corrupt data, get it restored and move forward from there.

To set up a backout plan consider the following:

>> What tool you're using and how to stop it from its intended actions.

>> If a tool is set in motion and starts to make changes, know what those changes are and how to fix what the tool may have damaged.

These points should all be documented in the change control document. Also, actively monitor the pen test so that you can identify when things go awry and be able to react to them immediately. If you're monitoring the tool and recording the outcomes in documentation for your after-action review of the scan, you can more likely identify when an issue takes place and be able to react to it immediately.

>> Ensure that any system you intend to scan has been identified as a system that has been backed up and or is resilient with some form of virtual backup or clone of the system. This way, if an issue takes place, the system or the system data can be restored immediately.

WARNING

As you conduct your pen test, if you find a major incident issue, you need to bring it to your leadership and stakeholder's attention immediately. Examples of this would be threats that if conducted could take down the entire environment and cause immediate loss to life, critical data, and or the operation itself.

IN THIS CHAPTER

» **Thinking like a hacker: infiltrating from outside**

» **Doing an inside job**

» **Keeping records**

» **Exploring other attack methods and vectors**

» **Looking over what you found**

» **Protecting against future attacks**

Chapter **10**

Conducting a Penetration Test

After you complete the preparation work that I cover in Chapter 9, you're ready to do a pen test! Here I take you through the process of the test and then look at the results of the assessment as well as methods of prevention.

In this chapter, I show you how to conduct a pen test in the following scenario:

» In the role as an outside security consultant for an organization.

» The organization wants assistance for the current staff in doing a risk and vulnerability assessment.

» Additionally, you'll ethically hack their systems to see where weaknesses exist in the current security posture.

TIP

If you've been skipping around in the book and haven't read through Chapter 9, go ahead and do that before going further in this chapter. That chapter covers a lot of the administrative issues required to pen test regarding permissions, documentation, legal matters, change process and management, and so on.

WARNING

Always be absolutely careful when you're working on a live network in production. Even better is to use a lab to learn how to conduct a pen test prior to doing it on a live network. In the spirit of measure twice and cut once, please make sure you are careful.

Attack!

For this pen test you will be starting at the network edge externally and attempting to make your way inside via any weaknesses found outside the network perimeter. I will go over each portion of the pen test so you can see a building block approach that you can adapt to future projects. Successful attacks might differ regarding your intentions and methods, but each successful attack essentially contain these actions, which happen in this order and which you'll mimic during a pen test:

1. **Infiltration.**

   Just gaining access is fairly easy and straightforward where those with access to hacking tools such as script kiddies can basically run attacks all day probing your defenses, looking for ways in and if they are lucky enough . . . get in.

   This means that an attacker had to be connected to the technology that they want to exploit. You want to make sure that you test and scan for vulnerabilities that disallow anyone who is unauthorized to connect to a network they don't belong to. This should at least minimize the amount of attacks just by who is able to sneak past and connect with this first level of security. Defense in depth should start to thwart an attack. Make sure that you disallow login access from devices that can be probed in this fashion. An access control list (ACL) can be configured on the device to tell it to only allow access from trusted IPs.

2. **Penetration.**

   Once access is gained, another level of access can be gained. This hop-by-hop strategy is used by more experienced hackers who can gain access (via malware as an example in the form of a Trojan horse) and then launch another attack or move to another segment of your network looking for more access or data.

   By attempting to spoof, connect, gain access, raise, and escalate privilege, assume the roles of other systems, and get in the middle of conversations the attacker is able to potentially do a vast amount of damage. An attacker could have run an APT and conducted eavesdropping that may have provided them more passwords or data. By running tools such as Burp Suite, Nessus, and Wireshark you can assess these vectors and ensure that access is limited in this area.

3. **Exploit.**

   At this stage, the hacker builds upon the previous level where access and access to data is actually achieved or granted and something of value can be garnished from the attack.

   Exploit is when the attacker has conducted the attack to gain and assume control; however, the next step would be to actually do the exploit. Steal data, take credentials, lay in wait for an APT, and do what they do. You can conduct similar attacks to see whether tools can flag these types of attacks taking place and how the security team can better monitor (and respond) to them.

4. **Conduct an advanced persistent threat.**

   The final level of this multilevel attack is the APT. To gain access, maintain it, have the ability to move around, and eventually gain access to valuable data while being undetected is the most valuable attack of them all.

5. **Exfiltration.**

   If they're able to do the previous steps and vanish without a trace, they have been highly successful in their attack.

TIP

You want to do the same as a pen tester and see whether you can set up ways to identify whether someone has been in the system without your knowledge. In the scenario with Company X, finish your pen test with an exfil and see whether any systems picked up a trace of your ability to access.

REMEMBER

Chapter 9 takes you through the preparations necessary to conduct pen testing: the preliminary logistics, the requirements gathering, and the planning. Although I guide you step by step through the pen testing process in the coming sections, you will benefit from reading that chapter before continuing here.

Infiltration

Company X, a technology company publicly traded on the market, is a medium-to large-sized company with approximately 10,000 employees.

The target will be data held internally, such as trade secrets on new technology development (research and development) that may be awaiting patents, sales data, or marketing information that has yet to be released to the public. You know the name of the company, and you want to launch a pen test to see whether you can find where this data may be located and/or saved. Here are the steps (and remember to document what you do and what you find as you go):

1. **Find out where the data is stored.**

    For the example of Company X, you'd do the reconnaissance work I describe in Chapter 2. You discover that the corporate data center and its mirror are in Colorado and Texas.

2. **With location information in hand, track down the phone numbers at the main site and start probing from spoofed phone numbers.**

    You can simply call the help desk and claim to be an internal resource looking to open a ticket and gain helpful information, such as source IPs (so you can get an actual IP address range for the internal network) and some other target information.

3. **To gain access externally, use the WhoIs database for DNS and locate a public IP address that you may be able to scan.**

    Figure 10-1 shows an example of looking up public information to gain some valuable insight when trying to find an attack vector. Here, if I run a search on a domain, I may be able to find their name servers that may be located on their network. Not all companies do this, but this might provide a clue.

FIGURE 10-1:
Doing a WhoIs
search to
gain intel.

4. Run a ping (like the one shown in Figure 10-2) to get the IP address from the domain name.

5. Start to run Nmap or another tool against that IP.

The goal is to find a public IP address or range to scan with your network mapper, such as Kali or Nmap, which can help to give you some access into the network.

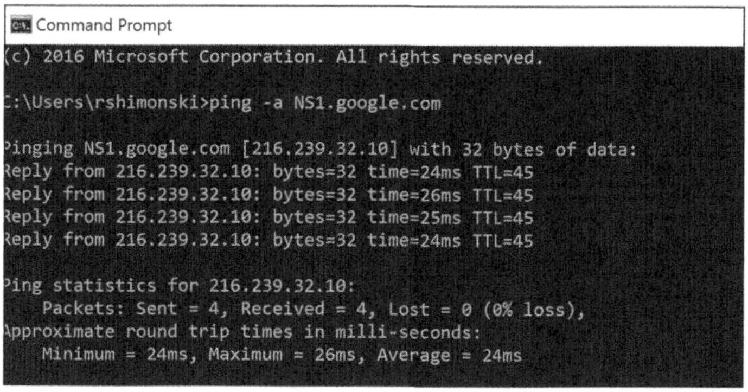

```
Command Prompt
(c) 2016 Microsoft Corporation. All rights reserved.

C:\Users\rshimonski>ping -a NS1.google.com

Pinging NS1.google.com [216.239.32.10] with 32 bytes of data:
Reply from 216.239.32.10: bytes=32 time=24ms TTL=45
Reply from 216.239.32.10: bytes=32 time=26ms TTL=45
Reply from 216.239.32.10: bytes=32 time=25ms TTL=45
Reply from 216.239.32.10: bytes=32 time=24ms TTL=45

Ping statistics for 216.239.32.10:
    Packets: Sent = 4, Received = 4, Lost = 0 (0% loss),
Approximate round trip times in milli-seconds:
    Minimum = 24ms, Maximum = 26ms, Average = 24ms
```

FIGURE 10-2:
Pinging at a command prompt to get an IP address or range to scan.

Penetration

6. Once in, find a way to access your targets.

The target in this case is internally held data. Some of the easiest and most common ways to get the data are these:

- *Deploy a piece of malware into the network via email or other means.* When users click it, you can gain access to their machine via a Trojan horse and from there you can control it like a zombie to do more reconnaissance work.

- *Brute-force attack a router (as an example) on the edge of a network you're scanning to see whether you can gain access by password cracking.* In this scenario, say a router is left with HTTP configured and you can probe it with Kali's xhydra, as shown in Figure 10-3. Using this tool, you can find the router's username and password and can now enter and gain access.

7. Once access is gained, get console access and then telnet or SSH to the device.

The goal here is to use the device as a springboard into the next target that you identify.

8. When you have console access, look at the routing table, ARP table, configuration, and other items to develop a manual map of what can be seen.

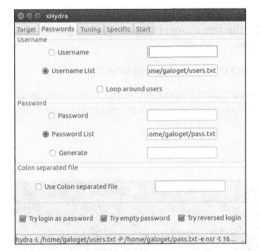

FIGURE 10-3:
Using Kali (Xhydra) to crack a router password.

Exploitation

9. **Start to scan, map, and identify the rest of the network looking for assets.**

In Figure 10-4, I have created a manual map of what I think I can get to from this first router hop.

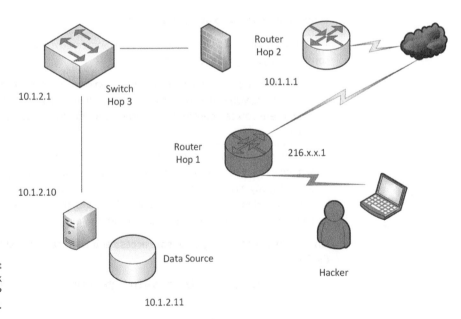

FIGURE 10-4:
A network map with IP addressing.

APT

10. **Begin an APT, a long-term engagement.**

At this point in the test, you have done enough to begin an APT — you can lay dormant inside the network and remain undetected for the purpose of continuing research and removing more information.

From moving from one device to another I have found that there is a Unix server (which looks like a dual node cluster; refer to Figure 10-4) at 10.1.2.10 and 10.1.2.11. Here I believe I have probed ports and found a possible database port open that I may be able to gain access to.

Exfiltration (and success)

11. **Get out.**

You have successfully gained access using tools from basic identification of a possible entry point, built a map, and found a potential database that you can continue to manipulate to get more (hopefully valuable) data.

At this point, you have proved enough that this pen test was successful and can disconnect from the system or get out by shutting down the tool or connection to the system.

Next steps

Although I made it look like this hack took about five minutes to do, it can take much longer than that. It may take a week to get valuable information that allows you to probe a perimeter network with a public IP address. It may take days to crack a router if it is even set up to answer to non-specified IPs it doesn't know. It can take a long time to get to the next hop, which you may not be able to reach as well.

After you get through these edge devices, you may have a firewall that tracks your movement or flags you as a threat. Host intrusion detection system (IDS) applications such as Tripwire may flag your probes of a critical database system that required priority protection.

This attack may take a long time (for many reasons) for anyone to perform when coming from the outside in. Many hacks come from the inside because, when there is an avenue inside to take, it reduces time and effort just in gaining access. Can it be done? Absolutely, and that is why you do vulnerability assessments and pen tests to find and close every single one of the holes you identified.

What would detection look like if you are caught in the system mimicking a hacker? Well, because you're performing a test, you would likely have given notice that you would be in the system. However, if running a test undetected, you stand the same chance any hacker would in being caught in a system and either terminated (your connection) or left alone based on the protocols of the incident response team.

Looking at the Pen Test from Inside

In the previous section, I look at a pen test (an attack) from the outside in. Here I talk about what it looks like if the attack comes from the inside.

First, if you're not a trusted user, you may have the same problems as you did from an external standpoint. You may not be able to immediately join a network without being identified by the same systems, like IDS. But you may be able to gain access differently.

For example, I may be able to simply plug into an open port on the network, be given a DHCP address, and away I go. I can open a console on either a Linux, Apple, or Windows desktop and start to look at the IP address I was given and then the default gateway, which is also the first router hop in the chain of attacks (as I outlined before).

If all ports are closed and unavailable, I may be able to gain access via joining a wireless SSID and attaching to a network running the same probes I did before, but most enterprise organizations separate their wireless systems into private and guest. Although anyone can generally join as a guest, what a guest can access is usually very well isolated from the corporate network, and you will find it incredibly difficult to find good information on the guest network.

You can also find an unattended workstation on which someone is still logged in with credentials and use that as a springboard. Using this method, you can even find users who have administrative or elevated privileges, enabling you to gain access to not only application information (which may expose where key systems are located on the network), but also possibly to the classified data you may be looking for. These methods are more manipulative and involve social engineering and trickery.

Documenting Your Every Move

Up until now you should be documenting (and should continue to document) everything you're doing. I show you with the map (refer to Figure 10-4) I devised from the information I was able to glean. Documentation is part of the reporting process I discuss in Chapter 11. The report is what you deliver to leadership, owners, stakeholders, and anyone invested in your test, rallying around you to help fund fixes, give resources, or help in your mission. In this section, I discuss network maps, the risk register, and how to stay balanced regarding what you find and what you recommend. (Chapter 12 covers recommendations.)

Network mapping

After gaining access, the next task any hacker or pen tester would do is create a network map, as I show in the "Exploitation" section, earlier in this chapter. The map is a fundamental building block and the biggest step towards a successful APT because it is a roadmap to those advanced attacks and hacks. It also offers a wealth of information that you will include in your report.

Starting with Nessus, you can run a vulnerability assessment to find holes in the network that you can crawl into. As shown in Figure 10-5, you should plug in some of the IP addresses you find (perhaps that database cluster you were able to identify) and let Nessus expose what may be wrong with it, what vulnerabilities exist, what patch levels are configured, and more. Once you review this, you can pull information needed to launch more attacks. For example, you may need to look for an open port and IP address combo to gain socket access into a target's resources. These clues can help you launch that attack to test and see whether it's possible.

If it is, the hackers can do it, too, so note it on your reports and add it to the risk register.

FIGURE 10-5:
Building a network map with Nessus.

You can run the same with Nmap, as shown in Figure 10-6. Once this scan is complete, you review the report, run the same tests, and add the appropriate information to the risk register.

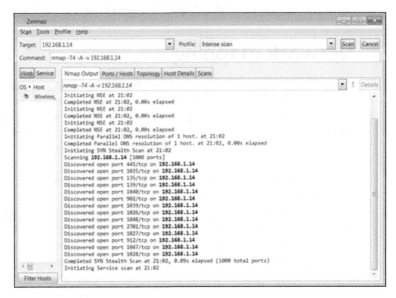

FIGURE 10-6:
Building a
network map
with Nmap.

Updating the risk register

You need to document risk carefully as you run your tools. At this point of your pen test you should be able to see that patches are missing, any critical AV software that is damaged, ports that have been left open that should not be, or critical systems that are unable to detect that you were there. What is at risk are the critical data, reputation, finances, and so on. All of these goes into assessing risk while you're mapping. They go hand in hand. I cover the risk register in more detail in Chapter 11.

Maintaining balance

You can't secure everything. You can't make everything bulletproof. The open nature of systems and the Internet and having the ability to access resources and use them will always leave some form of hole in your security plan. I always tend to explain that there is a need for balance and security needs to be applied by necessity.

This is true while conducting your assessment. While you pen test, you will obviously be able to knock on doors and they may even open. Some of this may be intentional by design so that it can provide a service, such as port 80 allowing HTTP traffic to flow so people can use the web. It may be the default administrator account for Windows left active and set up as a honeypot to audit attempts against it.

It may help to show you as a security analyst that there are potential threat actors trying to probe. Regardless, it goes into your map and it goes into your reporting, which both feed the risk register.

Other Capture Methods and Vectors

Not all pen testing should be done with a technology asset or tool. I urge you to employ other capture methods and vectors that require trickery, such as eavesdropping, skimming, screen surfing, social engineering, breaking and entering (with permission!), and dumpster diving. I describe some of these methods in Chapter 2, where I discuss upfront reconnaissance hackers do, but you can do them later in the process, too.

Scanning, doing assessments, probing, and network mapping will show you what your options are. Then, you can start to assume an identity and either spoof an address or poison an arp cache. From there, you can conduct MiTM attacks, replay attacks, eavesdrop, and assume the identity of others.

So, what other attacks could be present that takes a different vector or throws a cog in the machine you are aware of? Router hopping and wireless access are two, but what about coming in through a VPN access device? What about other remote access options? There are many other vectors to assess such as wireless, wired, mobile, VPN, dial up, and more, so make sure you look at them all.

Assessment

After you conduct a pen test, you move into assessment and reporting your findings. Throughout this section, I focus on assessing the results of the Company X pen test and ethical hacking from this chapter. However, I also note when what you're looking differs during certain types of attacks—such as the attacks I discuss in Chapters 5–8 — and what you might see in other pen testing scenarios.

Infiltrate

In an infiltration, an attacker had to be connected to the technology that they want to exploit. Pen testers will want to make sure they work to test and scan for vulnerabilities that will disallow anyone who is unauthorized to connect to a network they do not belong to.

This should at least minimize the number of attacks just by who is able to sneak past and connect with this first level of security. If applying defense in depth, your efforts should start to thwart an attack. Make sure you disallow login access from devices that can be probed in this fashion.

I also mention earlier that a router allowed a connection from an IP address it didn't know. An access control list (ACL) can be configured on the device to tell it to only allow access from trusted IPs.

>> **Overwhelm and disrupt:** The overwhelm and disrupt attacks I discuss in Chapter 6 don't always rely on stealth operations. Unless they're conducted internally, there is very little use for infiltration. There is also very little information gathering other than network mapping to identify target victim hosts.

Pen testers will want to make sure that they work to test and scan for vulnerabilities that will disallow anyone who is unauthorized to connect to a network they do not belong to and map it. If an attacker can't map your network, they will be hard pressed to overwhelm it. This doesn't mean this information cannot be gathered in other places.

>> **Subvert:** Based on the findings from subvert style attacks, which I discuss in Chapter 8, one of the biggest things you need to assess is that undetected system access can be the biggest threat because you don't know it's happening. If you do learn, it's usually too late, and the data has been offloaded from your systems.

Penetrate

By attempting to spoof, connect, gain access, raise, and escalate privilege, assuming the roles of other systems, and getting in the middle of conversations, the attacker is able to potentially do a vast amount of damage. In the example test in this chapter, I could have run an APT and conducted eavesdropping, which may have provided me with more passwords or data that could be used.

REMEMBER

By running tools such as Burp Suite, Nessus, and Wireshark you can assess these vectors and ensure that access is limited.

- **Overwhelm and disrupt:** Penetration comes in the form of the attack itself. Most times, if you're experiencing a distributed attack in the form of a flood, penetration has taken place using protocols and technology that was meant to be used, and, in most cases, can't be turned off (such as with ICMP and smurf attacks). Here, you need to monitor and assess the penetration. This is how you can test with the tools highlighted in Chapter 6.

- **Subvert:** Many other attack types (such as the destroy attacks in Chapter 7) can be leveraged during penetration when attention is subverted elsewhere. Now, once access was granted, data offloaded and clear, why not cause some problems by deleting some files? Or, hackers may delete something that causes you to look in one place while they're busy offloading data from another.

Exploit

Exploit is when the attacker has conducted the attack to gain and assume control; the next step is to actually do the exploit: that is, steal data, take credentials, lay in wait for an APT, and so on. Pen testers can conduct similar attacks to see whether tools can flag these types of attacks taking place and how the security team can better monitor (and respond) to them.

In the case of an overwhelm and disrupt attack, an exploit occurs when the attacker has conducted the attack and successfully disrupted your operation. If your company's web page is inaccessible because nobody can access it due to a DoS, the exploit has been successful. This is but one very common attack vector and type but one that has been perpetrated many times over the years by high-level hackers. It can be and has been carried out by very low-level script kiddies reusing tools they found on the dark web.

Exfiltrate

Exfiltration is a big win for an attacker. If they're able to infiltrate, penetrate, and exploit, and then vanish without a trace, they have been highly successful in their attack. You want to do the same as a pen tester and see whether you can set up ways to identify whether someone has been in the system without your knowledge.

In the scenario with Company X, you would end your pen test with an exfil and see whether any systems picked up a trace of your ability to access.

- **Overwhelm and disrupt:** For DoS attacks, exfiltration comes in the form of not being found in the first place — normally by spoofing or by using zombies to conduct the nefarious business.

>> **Destroy:** If a hacker successfully exfiltrates after the destruction of resources, consequences can be minimized if you have an active backup. If the source data/code is destroyed, and you don't have a backup, you lost. Some data that's lost while in transit (prior to backup) will be lost forever.

You might think that when you've concluded your testing, you will be aware of the risks. Those you were not aware of (as with logic bombs, which I cover in Chapter 7) can still cost you. You lose time and reputation, too, but your biggest cost (if you have a valid backup) is the time to restore systems. Other costs to consider with your assessment and report are any associated with the reinstall of systems, images, reapplication of data, and so on.

If you find that you need to patch 2,000 systems, part of what you need to assess is what it would take to later restore 2,000 systems if the patching isn't done.

>> **Subvert:** You can lose a lot with a subvert attack — data, trade secrets, privacy, reputation (maybe the biggest cost), information. A great example is if a healthcare network is attacked and patient data is stolen. This opens the affected company to lawsuits and loss of consumer trust over privacy concerns.

When you conclude your assessment after a subvert attack, you will have identified the issues discussed in Chapter 8. But you must remember that other attacks are sometimes used as a distractor to a multi-prong attack in which a hacker launches an APT while you're scrambling to handle the chaos of a logic bomb or malware.

Prevention

After you complete your assessment and report your findings to stakeholders, there needs to be a conversation around prevention. Throughout this section, I focus on general prevention best practices — hardening, monitoring, and of course retesting (see Chapter 13 for more about that). However, I also touch on specific ways to prevent attacks that I discuss in earlier chapters, notably over-whelm and disrupt (Chapter 6), destroy (Chapter 7), and subvert (Chapter 8).

Hardening

Take the time to look at the tools you used and the attacks you conducted as part of your pen test, using these tips as a guide to get you started:

- **>> Research vendor websites.** Look up the technologies in use and see what vendors recommend. For example, if you're using Microsoft technologies, there are literally thousands of documents online at Microsoft's website that show you how to tighten your security of its technologies. It may be the application of a bug fix, service pack, hotfix, new tool, removal of a service or additional of a service.

- **>> Harden your systems without breaking or restricting their functionality.** This balance may be hard to achieve because you will find that you can in fact harden something so much that it may not be useable.

- **>> Test and retest.** Harden your system and re-conduct the pen test.

Active monitoring

Another great method of prevention is to do active monitoring. If you're consistently monitoring the use of systems and their activities, you will be able to baseline those activities and hopefully able to spot anomalies when they occur. These may be flagged as possible attacks.

Retesting

As I mention in the "Hardening" section, never stop testing. There needs to be active updates to all systems in the form of new hardware, new firmware, updated software, and operating systems. Even drivers for devices need updates. Every time this takes place, the possibility for threat has been exposed. Do the updates, and then retest.

Devising best practices from lessons learned

The most effective best practices you can follow are from lessons you learn by testing in real environments. Reading alone can help but the more you touch the tools, test environments, and review the results, you eventually begin to generate more knowledge. By analyzing real attacks, you can learn from past tests (and perhaps mistakes) to help you use prevention best practices to keep the systems you're responsible for safe and secure.

Overwhelm and disrupt

It's possible to block many of the overwhelm and disrupt attacks (see Chapter 6) and mitigate risk of DoS by:

>> Patching your systems as necessary.

>> Distributing and ensuring malware detection such as antivirus software is updated and functional.

>> Blocking traffic at key points on routers and firewalls such as ICMP threats. Monitor for them and put alarms in place with intrusion prevention and detection systems to alert you of suspicious traffic patterns.

Destroy

Regarding destroy attacks, prevention comes in the form of knowledge. If your systems, tools, and protective software all remain updated, scanning for and seeing problems in your reports assist in the next steps of mitigating them.

This list highlights ways to help you prevent destroy attacks, which are often launched via malware getting into your systems and infrastructure:

>> **Educate users.** Some companies have multiple issues where pen testing can't reach the endpoint devices such as tablets and phones. Now, you can log into your corporate email from your mobile, and your pen test tools may not be able to reach them. Nobody should open unsolicited email attachments and links.

>> **Back up critical data.** You can prevent destroy attacks, but you also can recover from them. This means you must have good backups of your critical data.

>> **Consider user system rights and permissions.** Some pen test tools can identify whether users have elevated rights to install software. That should be identified and removed because that's the easiest way a virus can spread.

>> **Block malware.** At the highest level (and what you can also check as a pen tester) would be to identify whether your enterprise infrastructure is set up to block the ability for destroy attacks by stopping malware from coming through email by blocking it through filtering. Other ways to block malware:

- Use antivirus software and keep it updated and functional.

- Patch your systems as needed.

- Block traffic at key points on routers and firewalls for attacks such as malware. Monitor for them and put alarms in place with intrusion prevention and detection systems to alert you of suspicious traffic patterns.

Subvert

Similar to preventing destroy attacks, preventing subvert attacks relies on knowledge. If your systems, tools, and protective software all remain updated, scanning for and seeing problems in your reports can assist in the next steps of mitigating them.

As with destroy attacks, malware is used in subvert attacks. Refer to the bullets on educating users, user permissions, and blocking malware in the preceding section, "Destroy," as those points apply here, too.

Other ways to prevent subvert attacks is to consider blocking all ports and access found during scans from tools like Nessus. Also block access to privileged accounts and set up honeypots (an account used as bait).

4

Creating a Pen Test Report

Chapter **11**

Reporting

When you conduct pen tests, you will likely expose at least some weaknesses and vulnerabilities. The next step then is to report on your findings. In this chapter, I show you how to create a professional report to deliver those findings.

The goal of reporting is to focus on what needs to be done. You determine what needs to be done based on the project scope. It can be hard to manage this when you think of security holistically. Remaining vigilant and maintaining a high security posture requires applying defense in depth (the concept that, if you want to secure something, you consider all ways it can be exploited and add layers of security accordingly). You don't want to clutter your report, but at the same time, you need to be thorough and note any critical issues you find.

REMEMBER

The one major difference between the bad guys hacking and the good guys hacking (ethically) is reporting on what you find. The reports you create in the end ensures the work you do can help to create a program that strengthens security in your organization as a whole. And that helps to keep the bad guys out.

Structuring the Pen Test Report

Your report should come from a combination of the tools you use (some generate reports) and your own written work to explain overall health of the environment. A report comprises any sections outlined in the scope of the project (see Chapter 9), but this list shows sections that commonly appear:

>> **Executive Summary:** The executive summary briefly summarizes all of the key details of the report. It will speak to the reader in a way that lets them know what steps were taken, what the report ultimately found, and an overview or highlight of next steps, which might include recommendations (see Chapter 12).

>> **Tools, Methods, and Vectors:** This section covers the tools you used and the methods you chose to conduct the pen test. In addition to providing a general outline or narrative of your ethical hacks, also detail the paths you took with detailed step-by-step attack patterns and selected vectors.

>> **Detailed Findings:** This is where you will list all security risks, vulnerabilities, penetration points, threats, and concerns. Include the technical aspects of each finding in detail.

>> **Conclusion:** This section of the report reiterates the executive summary but with a focus on the next steps.

>> **Recommendations:** Although your job is ultimately to do the pen test and assess the health of the organization's overall security posture, you might be additionally responsible for providing guidance on ways to improve the security. If so, put those in a separate section and be as detailed as possible.

>> **Appendix:** Include this section for charts, logs, and any information that falls outside the project scope but which you think could be helpful.

This list shows how some reports are structured to give you a starting point. Your company may have specific ways in which they would like you to report, or you can find other examples online that can give you more ideas to choose from.

Executive Summary

The first part to consider in your report is your Executive Summary. A summary becomes an executive summary when you conduct a summary response in an organization that is likely read by the executive leadership staff.

For those of you who work in these environments, many times you have very little time to speak with and meet with senior executives so think of the executive summary as an elevator pitch. You need to very quickly and concisely talk to your goals, outcomes, and provide a high-level view of key findings. Keep details for the body of the report, not in the summary.

Overall, the goal of the summary is to let the reader know what steps were taken, what was ultimately found, and next steps. If these are the details of a pen test, an executive summary might look like what's shown in Figure 11-1:

> A companywide issue with all Apache web servers that can be accessed remotely without a required patch (more suited for the body in findings).

> You have or had a goal to identify whether your company-wide web architecture was secure for the upcoming holidays because the company relies on the integrity of these systems to be profitable in the fourth quarter.

FIGURE 11-1: An example executive summary.

Executive Summary
As requested by Company X, a pen test was requested to ensure the security posture of the web architecture was in fact sound in light of recent concerns made internally by IT professionals. It is critical that there would be no issues and that security would remain high during fourth quarter sales and the upcoming holiday season.
While conducting a pen test of this architecture, the following was found: • 42 identified risks added to the risk register. • 37 identified risks can be completely mitigated by XX/XX/XX. • The remaining 5 risks are acceptable risks and will be monitored.
As of the completion of this test and report, it has been deemed that once all risks have been mitigated, the security posture will remain high through the end of the year as expected and requested.

This (as noted) is only a suggestion; however, it fits all audiences. I didn't get into details about patches, vendors, systems names, technical jargon or any other albeit important, but unnecessary information for the executive summary. Those details can be added into other sections and appendices.

Another one of the biggest items to consider for the executive summary is scope. This should read very clearly in the first part of your report. I covered that a scan was needed and completed. I didn't get into what vectors I chose, tools used, methods and so on. I had to identify the web architecture because that was in scope. I didn't have to scan every part of and pen test the entire enterprise's technical footprint. The scope of the pen test was to identify whether security posture was high on the web architecture, and that's what I included in the summary.

Tools, Methods, and Vectors

This section of the report is where you can get more detailed, covering the tools that were used, what methods were chosen to conduct the pen test, paths taken, attack patterns, vectors selected. You can also write a general outline or narrative of the ethical hacks.

Figure 11-2 shows an example. You can either detail or map the specifics of what paths or vectors you took, what tools you used, and any specific methods of attack. This can be considered the attack narrative.

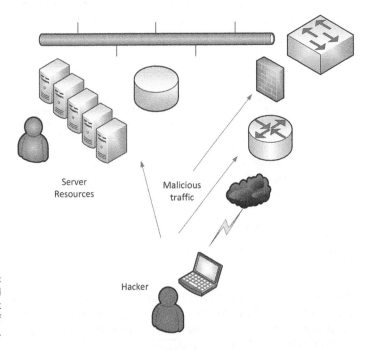

FIGURE 11-2:
Documenting and
reporting attack
vectors is part of
your narrative.

Figure 11-3 shows an example of what this section may look like.

Depending on the length and complexity of the pen test, this section can continue on with a step-by-step (or hop-by-hop) layout of the attack narrative and how certain information was found based on the assessment. The specifics here can really help to build a technical map for other teams you might collaborate with to address the risks.

Tools, Methods, and Vectors

After receiving specific infrastructure from Company X on initial infrastructure that needed to be protected at www.companyx.com, the next steps included:

- Conducting reconnaissance
- Collecting information to use for launching an initial attack

Once the public IP address space was identified that resolved to www.companyx.com and local DNS infrastructure was mapped out, the next steps were to run a vulnerability assessment using Metasploit Pro, which produced a report showing the following:

- Vulnerabilities in the TCP/IP stack of host x.x.x.x
- Open ports for SQL and DNS zone transfers

The possibility of attempting SQL injection was identified and became the next target to assess.

The attack vectors are highlighted in Figure 1.

FIGURE 11-3: An example of a Tools, Methods, and Vectors section.

You should always assume other technical teams (with permission of course) may be reading your report to help mitigate the risks. You are the pen tester, but the system administrator will likely be the one who needs to patch the DNS server that's providing zone transfers. The report findings may need to go to the SQL database administrator (or developers) who can help to fix the DBs to stop injection. These folks work with the risk register to close out the items prior to retest.

Detailed findings

All security risks, vulnerabilities, penetration points, threats, and concerns with a list of all technical aspects of each finding are provided in detail. This is the part of the report that allows you to really dig deeply into the specifics of your findings.

If you were able to penetrate a specific port and IP address combo or thwart a router's security, all that should go into detailed findings. You can also use the notes created and the tools report and audit output for help building your main report as shown in Figure 11-4.

The biggest difference between this section and the one previous is that this is where you can place the items identified and outcomes from the attack narrative. In this example, you may want to use the Metasploit audit logs to show all the vulnerabilities identified. You may want to show the specifics of the logs (in minute detail) where you found the zone transfer issue. You should show all details; however, if it seems to be too much information, you can choose to summarize for the sake of brevity. I would encourage you, though, to be cautious so you don't remove information that is needed for your report.

Major Findings

Discovered Operating Systems

Operating System	Hosts	Services	Vulnerabilities
iOS	2	2	0
Linux	2	9	0
Unknown	7	189	0

Discovered Hosts

Discovered	IP Address	Hostname	OS	Services	Vulns
8/22/19 1:39 PM	192.168.1.4	erikas-iPad.home	iOS	1	0
8/22/19 1:39 PM	192.168.1.102	192.168.1.102	Unknown	0	0
8/22/19 1:39 PM	192.168.1.9	192.168.1.9	iOS	1	0
8/22/19 1:39 PM	192.168.1.16	new-host-5.home	Unknown	0	0
8/22/19 1:39 PM	192.168.1.100	IP-STB1.home	Unknown	0	0
8/22/19 1:39 PM	192.168.1.101	IP-STB2.home	Unknown	0	0
8/22/19 1:39 PM	192.168.1.13	Rob-HP.home	Unknown	0	0

FIGURE 11-4: Include your main findings in your report.

It's these details that allows the technical teams to not only fix what you found in the pen test, but also identify any and all other issues that may be (or not) relevant to the conducted pen test. For example, your goal (in scope) may have been to protect web architecture, but the technical teams found that all of the Windows Servers are missing critical patches that help mitigate other issues that the tools may have found.

You don't want to overwhelm anyone, confuse the report, or stray too wildly from the goal/scope, but you're beholden to inform those of any and all security infractions you identify along the way. Cover those details that fall outside the project's scope in the appendices.

Conclusion

The Conclusion section takes everything you compiled into your report and succinctly wraps it up with a focus on next steps if any. Repeating what you wrote in the executive summary can be okay, as long as you switch the focus to next steps. You can of course outline next steps in the body or anywhere else in the report, but the conclusion at the end should take one last look at next steps holistically and purposefully. Figure 11-5 shows an example.

As you can see, the next step is to do a retest (which I cover in Chapter 13) to ensure that any documented changes, fixes, risk avoidance, or compliance items were handled and done so correctly. A retest will prove that.

FIGURE 11-5:
An example of a report conclusion.

Recommendations

As a pen tester you may need to supply some help to those who need it depending on the scope of the project or the size of the company. Smaller organizations may require you to help fix what you found and if you can, add this to your report. You can create a separate section or add it into the detailed findings.

As you will see, the detailed findings, appendices, and recommendations can be repurposed and reorganized based on what you need for your report. You could have a recommendations list in your appendix.

TIP

Recommendations should be made if they're in scope. Not all pen testers are required to recommend how to fix the items they found in the pen test. Should you know how to fix the items you have identified? If you want to learn more about security and how to be a better pen tester than the answer is yes, but it doesn't mean that it needs to be in the report you submit. If it is in scope then you should by all means create a list of items you believe that the company or organization should do to mitigate the risks you have identified. See Chapter 12 where I cover recommendations in detail.

Appendix/Appendices

Many reports might have extra information that may or may not be fully relevant to the scope or goal of your pen test and report. Place such information at the end of the report in an appendix or appendices (if you have multiples). Other information that can go here may be port charts, maps, full audit, or tool logs and other items that can be helpful to those using or reading the report.

Creating a Professional and Accurate Report

Writing the report isn't just about including the correct sections that I describe in the preceding section. You need to be professional, show correct data, and not mispresent findings. I've compiled this list of do's and don'ts to help ensure you deliver a great report.

Be professional

For the report itself, consider using company letterhead, or company branded office documents.

For the report out, which I discuss later in this chapter, consider using Power-Point, Keynote, or another presentation program to put your findings in a nice, visual layout.

Stay focused

The purpose of this pen test is to make sure you help an organization identify potential threats through analysis, assessment, and testing. You can then use a report to help develop mitigation strategies that can help with risk avoidance. If it's a major security concern, it may be a topic to broach but if it is not, it should be left out of your report.

Also, never steer away from what the purpose of your pen test is to meet your own needs or wants. You don't want to point out design issues that impact performance, vendor choices you may not like, or delve into areas outside of the intended purpose.

Avoid false positives

As you conclude your test and then your report, you need to ensure that your report has very carefully been cleaned up so that it doesn't misrepresent the outcomes of your test and it clearly depicts what needs to happen next. One of the items you want to ensure isn't in your report is unnecessary information. To take this topic one step further, you should ensure that you have inspected your data collection to filter any false positives from your report findings.

For those of you who are familiar with firewalls and firewall logs (as an example), if you look at the log output you can immediately get overwhelmed. That said, you may want to use snippets of information. You can also clean up the information in a way that highlights what you want the report reader to focus on.

Lastly, you don't want incorrect or erroneous information in the report. Because of that, you should do a data clean up (or sanitize the data) prior to using it. An example may be, if you're trying to show a log entry for someone entering FTP ports from an unauthorized IP address, you would want to remove any information from the authorized ones. These may show up as false positive information where the access was flagged and recorded, but it doesn't impose a threat and/or are relatable to the pen test and threat assessment.

Classify your data

Another important factor for your reports may be to consider doing a data classification exercise so that your report findings can be grouped for easy interpretation and easy assignment for remediation. For example, if you place your findings in categories such as subvert attacks, destroy attacks, or other examples provided in this book, you can also prioritize the threat level based on these findings.

The goal is to make sure that important data is easy to identify and assign. When attempting to ensure risk compliance, management, avoidance, and acceptance, you want to make sure you do not miss any priorities based on the outcomes from your pen test.

Encourage staff awareness and training

Your report should contain information that points to areas in your pen testing and ethical hacking that leads to a need for staff training and awareness. For example, if you were able to hack via social engineering, phishing, trickery, deception, or any other form of hack I cover in this book to subvert stealth attacks, you need to highlight these areas in your report as a need for training and awareness.

Delivering the Report: Report Out Fundamentals

After report creation comes delivery: This is the *report out,* and it should be reported to those who need to hear it, the stakeholders in your project or program. Who you will ultimately be reporting out to should be identified up front as part of the preparation I discuss in Chapter 9.

WARNING

As pen test reports can contain some highly sensitive (and sometimes dangerous) information, it's imperative you give your report to *only* those who need to know. Your findings should be considered secret unless you have permission to declassify them. Because the report essentially creates a step-by-step roadmap on how to get past very expensive security technology and steal company data, you should secure and perhaps even password protect or encrypt your report for safe keeping.

The report out follows the same structure as your report, with the same sections. Because you will be presenting your report during the report out, creating a presentation with slides helps you cover the appropriate talking points while showing the information in a clear, visual, and professional manner.

Updating the Risk Register

A report is just a document. It is what you do with the information in the report that matters. After you outline a series of remediations that need to take place, add them to the risk register and then prioritize them. The risk register, which I introduce in Chapter 2, is the database of risks that need to be worked on to lower risk, and those can be either risk aversion or risk avoidance specific.

As you scan, assess, penetrate, and test, you will find issues to add to the risk register. The report is created specifically for each test while the register is a living, breathing document that accompanies all post-test reports and that is continually updated. Risk registers generally include the risks and vulnerabilities you found, how you discovered them, the level of risk associated with each, and a priority for dealing with each. For example:

>> **Low-level risks:** The risk can be small where you know there is a problem, but you accept the risk of it being a problem because you might not be able to fix it at this time. Maybe a patch is not yet available by a software vendor, and you have to wait.

You might identify a risk and decide to monitor it, but if there is a penetration and exploitation of that risk, it will lead to very little threat. An example may be if the company's reputation is hurt slightly by upsetting a few clients who rely on the systems, but they were not available for the day. It was disruptive but not harmful to the clients. You might accept this as a low-level risk.

>> **High-level risks:** A high-risk item may be one that is likely to be exploited. And if it is, that may cause major financial losses for company, as well as a big negative impact on their reputation, or worse, a loss of life.

Dealing with the risk register is just part of being a pen tester, and it might require some project management on your part. Standard project plans with Gantt charts, critical paths, and assigned resources and tasks can be used. A company might prefer agile methods or a scrum team that uses scrum boards to assign resources and tasks. You'll get your remediation either documented post report or risks mitigated through task completion. Either way, be aware that this is an important part of the post testing/analysis/report out process.

Depending on what was established during the preparations (see Chapter 9), the process for dealing with risk mitigation might look something like this:

1. **Collect data and organize it into a report.**

2. **Map the identified risks into the risk compliance program.**

3. **Determine a fix.**

   An example may be the SQL injection attack identified in the pen test report. The fix may be to secure the database with patching, configuration, or additional security applied.

4. **Assign the fix.**

   Resource allocation is an important part of project management. You want to be sure whoever is assigned can handle the efforts before you attempt to rescan. There is no reason to retest if you know the vulnerabilities still exist.

5. **Go through the change control process to mitigate the issue.**

6. **Mark the item as complete and retest.**

   A retest will likely show this issue no longer exists. If a retest flags the issue again, it goes back into the report and the risk register item is reopened.

IN THIS CHAPTER

» **Exploring the need for recommendations**

» **Offering ways to shore up security**

» **Looking at general areas of security to strengthen**

» **Showing how to defend against attacks**

» **Understanding and protecting vectors**

Chapter **12**

Making Recommendations

I n this chapter, I try to capture the most common issues you might encounter and recommendations you'll likely want to make based on your tools. The chapter focuses on the tools, the report, the output, and your report findings and fuse those with best practices found in the industry today.

Most of what you find in this chapter (and in real life) is that most of the recommendations revolves around systems that are not up to date and need security and other forms of patching or misconfigurations that lead to security risks in your infrastructure, network, and applications.

This is your time to shine! You can highlight many of the items you will learn in your report, create a separate report or put a presentation together and/or give a training class or awareness seminar. All this is part of post-test assessment and recommendations that you can provide your company or clients based on your findings.

Understanding Why Recommendations Are Necessary

You may be given tasks where you just run the pen test, collect the findings, and report them. Other times, you are expected to recommend how to remediate some of the issues you've identified.

Before you report any recommendations, think about these key considerations:

» **Not all recommendations are actionable.** You'll find accepted risks (which are noted on the risk register), and you may have to have alternative solutions in place to mitigate the threat. For example, a router may need to remain exposed.

The recommendation normally would be to block access to the router. Because it needs to be accessed, hardening it with access control lists may be the viable solution in this case.

» **Some recommendations may not solve the problem.** You may make recommendations that are industry-standard solutions that often come from the vendors, but they may not mitigate the risk.

There may be more risks hidden within the solution. This is where retesting (which I cover in the next chapter) comes into play and is a critical piece of pen testing.

WARNING

If you're asked for recommendations, options, or solutions on security threats in an organization post pen test, be sure you're confident in your ability to do so. Your strengths may lie in pen testing but may not rely on applying security solutions in an enterprise. For example, some solutions might require programming to fix, and maybe you aren't a programmer. Be honest with your abilities and make sure you're honest with the project team. This is when other consultants or experts may be brought in to help apply the security solutions needed when others can't apply them. The role of the pen tester is to penetration test and ethically hack to find weaknesses. Another person (or team) might be responsible for securing the weaknesses. Whatever part you play in this process, you can learn from it and it will make you a better pen tester over time.

Seeing How Assessments Fit into Recommendations

When you're making recommendations, keep in mind you might need to consider information from various sources and that you might need to supply information to someone else. The latter case happens when you're only running the test and submitting a report, but another person or team actually makes the recommendations.

Here's where you most likely get information to build a recommendation list, if you're responsible for this task:

>> The assessments from the pen test you conducted

>> The final pen test report you submitted

>> Your pen test tool logs and any other artifacts you have from the test

>> An existing pen test report that you need to analyze

Your first steps are to review what you have conducted and start to develop a recommendations list from your reported findings.

In Figure 12-1 is a snapshot from Nessus that highlights findings I put into a report after a pen test. If I were to create a series of recommendations from this snapshot alone, I may come up with some of the most obvious, such as reviewing the organization's use of the Firefox web browser installed on Apple OS and whether an upgrade or a patch is needed. At this point, I'm getting the lay of the land if you will.

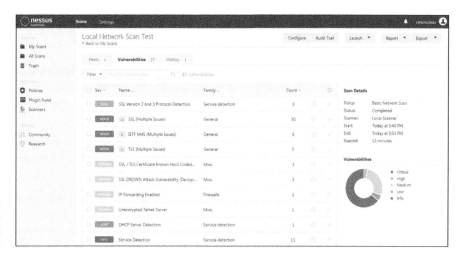

FIGURE 12-1:
Reviewing Nessus
for hardening
tips.

These are some of the easiest assessment-based recommendations to make because you have a blueprint to follow. You should also use the priority flags from the toolset to provide a priority level to each item for your risk register.

A recommendation to make here may also expand beyond a patch or a security update. You may do some research and find that the browser itself is flawed, it is unable to be fixed (perhaps it's not fixed by the vendor yet), and is so critical that you need to disable the use of this browser across your organization until it's fixed.

TIP

If you need to do additional research to fully understand a flagged issue and how it affects the organization, you might need to make more than just a general recommendation. The situation might call for a series of recommendations that could even spawn a new project or effort within the organization to mitigate the risk.

REMEMBER

Reconnaissance work can provide a lot of information. It may be hard to make a recommendation to keep a lower profile online, but it may be one you have to suggest. For example, in previous chapters, I show you how a pen tester might find a public IP address or a phone number to start attacks. You can attempt to keep all that information away from hackers, but that's likely not a viable option. Instead, heed this advice:

>> **Do your best to suggest a reduced footprint.** Reduce the amount of overhead in your technology that you may not need. For example, if you're using Windows systems and you don't need certain services, remove them or disable them. An example could be to turn off AutoPlay (AutoRun in older systems), which allows devices once connected to run what may be on them. AutoPlay is dangerous because anyone can plug in a USB drive with malware, which would immediately install. By turning off a service of this kind, you have reduced the attack service, reduced exposure, hardened your system, and inevitably reduced your footprint.

>> **Educate those who might be susceptible to providing sensitive information.** Social engineering, which I discuss further in Chapter 4, is a great way for would-be hackers to coax information such as usernames and passwords out of unwitting users.

>> **Keep certain information on a need to know basis.** People need access to information required to perform their jobs, so policies managing access should be in place.

>> **Become deceptive with what you provide as information.** For example, you might recommend turning a default account on a system into a *honeypot* to identify whether possible attackers are testing the waters from inside your organization. A honeypot account looks and behaves like the real account, but it's isolated from other systems, so no actual damage can be done if someone does hack into it.

Networks

Making recommendations to harden your network can come from the current pen test and report you conducted and completed. You may have found a series of ports open that allowed access to systems or credentials to devices that were easily cracked and accessed.

General network hardening

There are many ways to secure and harden a network:

>> **Use challenging password security options and block IP access from unknown sources.** Doing so helps you to protect and harden against router hopping from device to device. Hackers commonly try to breach a network by router hopping. You can use Kali to check routers for access and conduct brute force password cracking until access is gained.

>> **Use encryption.** Other attacks I covered include buffer overflows, reading routing updates that were left unencrypted, and more. Every one of these should be in your recommendations list and how they can be fixed so that the attack can't be conducted in the future, or if you can't block or change access, how to monitor for intrusion so you're aware if a hack is taking place.

>> **Disable any services not in use.** As mentioned earlier in the chapter, reducing the footprint or attack surface can minimize what a hacker has access to exploit. An example could be to remove any protocols not being used so if you are only using TCP/IP version 4, you can remove version 6. You can remove NetBIOS if you're only using DNS for name resolution and so on.

>> **Use up-to-date software that is free of bugs and security issues.**

>> **Leverage** *Authentication, Authorization, and Accounting* **(AAA) whenever possible.** AAA is used as a service that allows you to monitor access into devices so you can review a log of all activities taking place.

- *Authentication:* Authentication handles credentials such as username and password. Without a credential set, you can't access a system. You must authenticate to a system to use it.

- *Authorization:* Authorization gives you permission to do things. So, for example, your user account may belong to a group that allows you access to data.

- *Accounting:* Accounting is the log based on what you do once you've been authenticated and authorized (or not authorized) based on your activity. So, when you access the file, it appends to a log what you have done and makes inspection and tracking easier for those looking to protect services, systems, and data.

>> **Ensure certain attack patterns are nullified by additional security.** For example, applying SSH instead of telnet so passwords that aren't cleartext can be caught by pen test tools such as Wireshark, or further segmenting protected areas of your network with VLANs (virtual LANs) so that access can be controlled to secure services like databases you want to keep secure.

>> **Rely on vendors.** For example, Cisco Systems (`www.cisco.com`) is one of the premier vendors of network equipment and software. Cisco provides a hardening guide (as most vendors do) so that you know how to increase your security posture and allow for your systems to be in a higher state of protection then if you didn't apply many of the suggestions they make.

```
https://www.cisco.com/c/en/us/support/docs/ip/access-lists/13608-21.html
```

Also, many of these same suggestions (such as using a centralized log collection) can be further used and suggested on other systems regardless of make or vendor. Some of the suggestions are best practices no matter what product you use.

Network segmentation

Networks can be laid out in many ways, but most (if not all) generally follow basic standards. You can see most of them in Figure 12-2. The figure shows the most common, which is the division of the internal and external networks (usually by the demarcation of the public or private owned vendor network) that allows you to gain or get access into and out of your internal network. Along the external edge is where most hackers attempt to penetrate because this is where you're visible on the public Internet.

To access an internal company network, you have to use a public facing connection to then connect in from the edge into the company network to access their core. The *core* is commonly referred to as the high-speed center of any network that is configured.

Depending on the size of the network, you could say that most core networks at least have a distribution, or access, layer where other switches connect and wired and wireless segments connect together. Most of these segments are configured with different IP address blocks and further configured as virtual local area networks (VLANs). Segmentation (physically by device or logically by VLAN) can help you protect each portion with access lists or firewalls so you can control what people can or can't access based on what they're permitted to do.

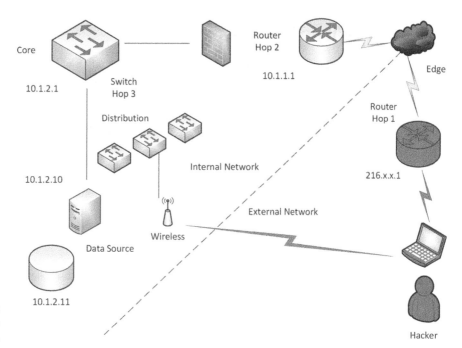

FIGURE 12-2:
A large
network map.

Within the figure:
- Core
- 10.1.2.1
- Switch Hop 3
- Distribution
- 10.1.2.10
- Data Source
- 10.1.2.11
- Wireless
- Internal Network
- External Network
- Router Hop 2
- 10.1.1.1
- Edge
- Router Hop 1
- 216.x.x.1
- Hacker

Internal network

Making recommendations to secure a local internal network are fairly straightforward:

>> **Make sure the recommendation is correctly documented.** This is true of any recommendation of any IT system or services. Documentation helps all parties better understand, respond to, secure, and operate their technology investment.

>> **Use IANA private IP addressing blocks and segment your network correctly.** Keep critical resources on private networks or VLANs that you can use your routers or layer 3 switches as barriers by controlling access with access control lists or only routing approved segments to these private ones. This step alone helps to mitigate many hop-by-hop attacks and stop many hackers in their tracks.

>> **Secure the core network by only allowing traffic to traverse it.** You don't necessarily plug servers directly into it as shown in Figure 12-2. This is one reason why it was so easy to access this server because it was further segmented into the distribution layer.

Wired/wireless

A major challenge with wireless networks is that they aren't always set up correctly. An example may be where a hacker is able to see and get a signal from a wireless access point from the external network (refer to Figure 12-2). This can be a hacker with a transmitter hacking from the parking lot with a high-powered antenna to see whether any SSIDs respond to beaconing.

If you show you can in fact gain access this way, here are a few recommendations to make:

>> Turn off SSIDs to private networks so they do not advertise.

>> Lower the decibel and power rating on the access point so it doesn't transmit past the walls of the organization.

>> Set up monitoring of the wireless network through controllers that allow for auditing and other AAA functions.

External

The external network is hard to secure because most times you don't own the systems that the ISP provides. You also need to consider that you are limited in what you can secure, but this is the true power of the pen test and the pen test report. If you find that you scan the provider and edge leading into your private network (the demarcation is considered the DMZ, or demilitarized zone) where you may even host public facing systems, you can show where they need to lock down their own system or if you own them, lock down your own.

Systems

Whether you pen test and report on Windows, Linux, Unix, Apple OS, or basically any other operating system in your organization, you will find some form of vulnerability that needs to be patched, fixed, reconfigured, or examined. With the nature of changing technology, there will always be updates that cause more problems later. Most, if not all, pen test output shows operating systems that need patching or protected against some form of threat in the wild.

WARNING

Keep in mind any compliance standards the organization must adhere to. These are most common in finance and health, but other industries might have compliance issues, too. Many operating systems are required to be compliant, so you will find information on vendor websites on how to bring a system *into compliance,* which means you are hardening it and thus you can add that to your list of suggestions.

REMEMBER

You can also find hardening suggestions and toolkits, such as the Microsoft Security Compliance Toolkit 1.0 at `www.microsoft.com`. This tool enables you to run configuration baselines for Windows products, so you can apply security to your systems as needed. Some compliance standards you may need to map to include — but are not limited to — PCI DSS compliance, NERC-CIP, NIST 800-53, and NIST 800-171.

In general, you can apply across the board some of these common guidelines:

>> **Apply hardening to the base operating system.** If you were considering Windows desktops (very commonly a big footprint in most organizations), you would want to consider focusing on Internet Explorer or Edge and using policies to control what it allows an end user to do.

>> **Include a program for patching and compliance**. The program should allow all Windows desktops to be up to date with all critical security patches most of which stop elevated privileged and malware.

>> **Lock down local administrator rights and privileges.** You limit access rights for any user, admin, or anyone permitted to use the system so that they only have rights to do exactly what they need to do.

TIP

Because default administrator accounts have access to literally everything, consider making them honeypot accounts to ensnare unsuspecting hackers looking to attempt to use them. Or disable them and give rights to the named accounts of your users and admins with logging enabled to ensure that no unnamed accounts remain in use with the power to do anything on your systems.

>> **Ensure the desktops use an updated antivirus program.**

>> **Stay abreast of new features available with newer versions of operating systems.** With these newer systems come updated forms of security, and you're responsible to know about these updates and consider recommending them if you find that you were able to penetration and exploit a system because it was not available. One example of this may be the Windows 10 Attack Surface Reduction (ASR) feature that can work with your AV solution against malware.

Servers

You secure servers by hardening them using vendor recommendations. For example, if you have a Windows Server system, a large number of services specific to that vendor are available. You must consider turning all those services on or shutting them off based on what you captured during your pen test.

To generalize, if you run Unix or Windows, you want to make sure that they are both not running extraneous services (like telnet) and secure them with SSH as an example.

No matter what you pen test (and report on), when you're making recommendations, include general or standard server recommendations and then you make those more specific. To further explain what I mean:

>> A general recommendation would be to make sure all your servers are patched to the approved level by the vendor and that all current security patches are applied.

>> A more specific recommendation would be to make sure that Company X shuts down and stops the DHCP server service found on a rogue Windows system that could inadvertently dole out IP addresses to unsuspecting victims.

You can follow these same recommendations for any server platform you choose to test.

Client-side

Client-side attacks are the most common because the desktop (and other desktop level devices) are the most commonly used, easily accessed, least protected and least monitored of all infrastructure components. They are the easiest to infiltrate with malware or even through social engineering.

The most common recommendations:

>> **Make sure client systems are patched and updated.**

>> **Run current AV software on the clients and ensure they're scanned daily.**

>> **The devices should be encrypted and unusable in case of theft or if lost.**

>> **Access to the devices should be secured through awareness training and constant reminder from IT staff.**

>> **Disable unneeded services.** As shown in Figure 12-3, one of the things you can do on server systems, client systems, and even routers and switches, is disabling unneeded services; for example, telnet.

The figure shows a command prompt window:

```
Administrator: Command Prompt                              —  □  ×
Microsoft Windows [Version 10.0.18362.175]
(c) 2019 Microsoft Corporation. All rights reserved.

C:\WINDOWS\system32>dism /online /Enable-Feature /FeatureName:TelnetClient

Deployment Image Servicing and Management tool
Version: 10.0.18362.1

Image Version: 10.0.18362.175

Enabling feature(s)
[==============================100.0%==========================]
The operation completed successfully.

C:\WINDOWS\system32>dism /online /Disable-Feature /FeatureName:TelnetClient

Deployment Image Servicing and Management tool
Version: 10.0.18362.1

Image Version: 10.0.18362.175

Disabling feature(s)
[==============================100.0%==========================]
The operation completed successfully.

C:\WINDOWS\system32>
```

Infrastructure

General infrastructure includes storage platforms, mainframes, tape silos, and anything else that falls outside of the network and servers attached to them. You need to consider each separately and harden it accordingly.

Some examples (and suggestions) include but aren't limited to all of these devices connect to the network that share network interfaces, ports, and protocols, use TCP/IP (or other protocol), and communicate and pass traffic back and forth. Because they do, every single one of them becomes a target to an unethical hacker or ethical hacker.

Storage systems might be considered the holy grail of data capture. Storage arrays normally host terabytes of data, the company's databases, and other critical data that keeps many technology-driven companies alive and healthy. To launch an attack and successfully destroy, overwhelm, or subvert any of this infrastructure is an immediate win.

The recommendations are similar to what I cover for networks and systems:

>> **Access (and follow) vendors' online hardening guides.**

>> **Make sure you have a working copy of your data in a redundant and resilient setup.** This is where disaster recovery (DR) and business continuity planning (BCP) become a pen tester's main suggestion to a client.

If you have the important data backed up and available, any issues to it can be solved.

REMEMBER

>> **Use some of the same recommendations given for network and systems.** To help you secure access against it, apply access control correctly, for example, and monitor (audited) for threats.

>> **Encrypt data.** Encryption of data both in transit and at rest can protect any data on the storage system, going to it or being requested.

Mobile

Mobile systems are increasingly hard to secure. Pen testing them is often more critical than pen testing an internal core network secured by firewalls. As I mention with client-side attack secure recommendations, earlier in this chapter, mobile fits directly into this model where all work and functions are performed on them are transported from place to place in an always-on configuration.

Mobile is normally secured by local biometric access or a password/passcode. Corporate devices face a current challenge with end users wanting to own and operate their own personal devices to access corporate resources.

Recommendations include:

>> Divide the access between personal and work use with a VPN, or other secure form of app that allows your corporate resources to remain secure. It also helps to prevent the spread of malware.

>> Find out what is being used on employees' devices and attempt to secure them with protective software and encryption.

Mobile pen testing can be as follows: You send an email to an end user who opens it on the Android phone (or jailbroken iPhone). This allows for an app to be installed, much like a Trojan horse. Access can be provided and from there you can launch attacks. If you know what apps are there, you secure them accordingly.

>> Use a mobile management enterprise solution if your company can afford one to manage this as well.

Cloud

Assessing cloud and other forms of outsources services that connect to your corporate company can be a true challenge. The truth is, though, it's not much different than other connectivity you may have, such as ISP connections and disaster recovery locations where you may host systems.

REMEMBER

The cloud is nothing more than an external network that you access and use from a provider, usually on a leased basis.

WARNING

Whether the solution you use is cloud based or internal, you should follow many of the same recommendations you would follow with your own internal networks, infrastructure, servers, systems, and applications. Just make sure you understand that they are leased; you and your company don't own them. You must gain permission to access them, scan them, test them, and/or secure them if needed.

General Security Recommendations: All Systems

From ports and unused services to firewalls and encryption (and more), this section covers several recommendations that don't fall specifically under networks and systems. Though general in nature, they're still important, of course, and so I take them one by one.

Ports

One of the most common items to appear on pen test reports is ports. Closing unnecessary server ports helps if you can't change them or readjust them. The IANA registry shows the list of commonly used and assigned ports:

```
https://www.iana.org/assignments/service-names-port-numbers/service-
names-port-numbers.xhtml
```

It's important to be aware of ports and how they're used and configured. Ports are commonly how attackers and pen test access remote systems through socket connection established by a port and IP address set. The example in Figure 12-4 shows one of the ways you can secure a system by changing the default port. Another consideration is, if Server A wanted to access web services on Server B, it would have to do so by specifying the port by number and look like: 10.1.1.11:8080.

Unneeded services

Remove unneeded services from systems and audit them periodically for use. What this means is, if you find that you have the FTP service running on most of your servers but FTP is only really needed on two of them, remove the unneeded ones.

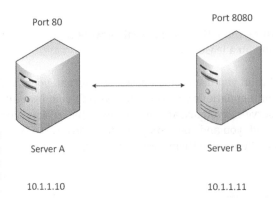

Port 80   Port 8080

FIGURE 12-4:
Changing a
default port to
help secure a
system.

Server A   Server B

10.1.1.10   10.1.1.11

A pen test and thus the pen test report can help guide you into removing these items. Often tools such as Nmap show you what ports are running and commonly map to which services are in use. This highlights what you can shut off.

A patch schedule

Make sure that every single piece of technology in your organization is on a patch program where everything is reviewed, tested, and applied as required on a monthly basis.

Firewalls

Installing a firewall is one of the most common things that organizations do to protect their demarcation point and control access to hosts that the company may manage in their DMZ. Figure 12-5 shows how monitoring access in and out of the firewall can be helpful to an organization trying to protect their assets. You can then audit the firewall log to see what connections were attempting to gain access to a specific server. Use that information to look for possible attacks or breaches.

AV software

Today, the only thing more important than using a firewall is to make sure all your devices use an active AV program such as the one shown in Figure 12-6. AV is one of the best ways to protect endpoints, client-side devices, and mobile from being flooded with problematic malware.

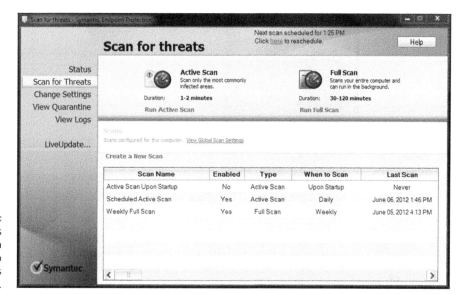

Severity	Syslog ID	Source IP	Source Port	Destination IP	Destination Port
i 6	725003	10.0.220.13	59043		
i 6	725001	10.0.220.13	59043		
i 6	302013	10.0.220.13	59043	10.0.0.1	4433
i 6	302020	10.0.220.13	11	10.2.2.36	0
i 6	302013	10.0.220.13	59041	50.19.236.61	80
i 6	305011	10.0.220.13	59041	12.178.152.131	59041
i 6	302013	10.0.220.13	59040	50.19.236.61	80
i 6	305011	10.0.220.13	59040	12.178.152.131	59040
i 6	106015	10.0.220.13	57973	10.0.0.1	4433
i 6	106015	10.0.220.13	57968	10.0.0.1	4433
i 6	106015	10.0.220.13	57967	10.0.0.1	4433
i 6	106015	10.0.220.13	57969	10.0.0.1	4433
i 6	106015	10.0.220.13	57971	10.0.0.1	4433
i 6	106015	10.0.220.13	57974	10.0.0.1	4433
i 6	106015	10.0.220.13	57972	10.0.0.1	4433
i 6	106015	10.0.220.13	57970	10.0.0.1	4433
i 6	106015	10.0.220.13	59038	10.0.0.1	4433

FIGURE 12-5:
Using a firewall allows you to monitor access in and out.

FIGURE 12-6:
Antivirus software is still an effective way to protect devices from attack.

Sharing resources

Another common recommendation is to disable services by blocking ports or disable sharing of resources that are not needed within the operating system you're hardening. For example, with Windows (and some Linux distributions), you can use SMB or SAMBA and share resources such as folder, printers, and so on. One of the ways malware propagates through a network from system to system is by riding these kinds of protocols.

In Figure 12-7, Nessus found SMB in use on the network and is recommending that you either shut it down (if possible) or configure much needed patches that disallow remote code execution.

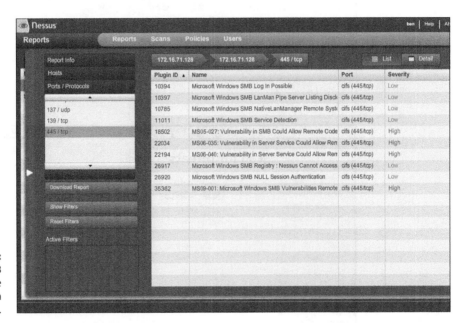

FIGURE 12-7:
Finding SMB issues on the network with Nessus.

Although you may need this protocol for file sharing and can't turn it off, you may want to ensure that it's patched correctly at minimum.

TIP

Encryption

Using encryption allows you to not worry about many of the common attacks such as eavesdropping, hijacking, data theft, and packet sniffing and capture. By using protocols, such as SSH, IPsec, and SSL/TLS, you can prevent many attacks through encryption, as shown in Figure 12-8.

Although you should use encryption whenever possible, it's not enough. You must ensure that you use *strong encryption*. Always recommend using strong encryption methods so that the weaker forms of encryption can't be cracked. See Chapter 4 for more about encryption.

REMEMBER

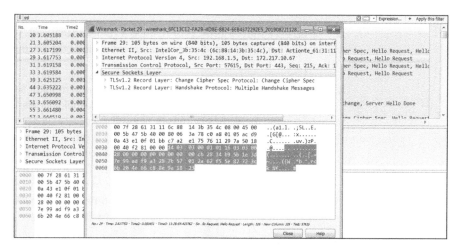

FIGURE 12-8:
Use encryption
such as SSL.

More Recommendations

This section gives you a quick snapshot of other important recommendations that didn't fit elsewhere in the chapter.

Segmentation and virtualization

One really important one is a different view on segmentation. You should always put more critical systems into separate parts of the network whenever possible. This doesn't just mean network components; it also means the systems that connect to your network such as servers. This can be more easily accomplished with virtualized servers (or virtual machines) within a virtualized host.

Also consider virtualization. With the use of VMware and other technologies you can also create virtual machines (VMs) that allows you to create separate logical networks instead of physical ones, much like VLANs.

Access control

Gaining access is one of the biggest targets for hackers (and pen testers), which makes access control where you can potentially thwart incoming attacks. Some of the recommendations you can make here is to

>> Use a tool for AAA, such as TACACS+ or RADIUS, which provides centralized logging and control of access.

>> Use access control lists (ACLs). An ACL is a guideline that your system must follow to permit access. If a deny statement is within the list, the system blocks entry.

>> **Use firewalls and firewall rules.** Firewalls can also monitor and log information for later review, or send alerts based on thresholds or alarms that are set to be tripped for alerting purposes. Firewall rules (very similar to ACLs) are statements that a system reviews when entry is requested and if a deny statement is used, it blocks entry based on specific criteria such as a port, IP address, hostname, or other form of identifier. The firewall can also be intelligent in that when it sees something out of the ordinary, it can send an alert to the administrator. For example if a port known for hacking is accessed on a system very rarely used, it may trigger the firewall to send an alert.

>> **Enforce secure password or credential usage.** A set of credentials is a username and password combo, unless you're using multifactor authentication mechanisms, biometrics, or other form of access and identity control.

- *Have multifactor authentication (MFA) in use.* MFA increases the difficulty of password guessing or cracking. It's especially true with the extra factor added is something like a one-time password (or OTP) that needs to be generated and used on demand.

- *Encourage strong passwords.* Another consideration is to have a password policy in place for your organization that disallows the use of easy to guess passwords and makes the end users change them in a specified amount of time.

- *Disable default, unnamed, or generic accounts.* You want to ensure that credential sets are tied to real users who can be audited. Any default accounts can be set up as a trap (for example, a honeypot) and audited so that if you do see activity on default (and honeypot) accounts, you know someone is probing the network or attempting to.

Backups

Creating and keeping backups is vital to the health of an organization. You can't continue operations if you lose critical data or systems with no way to access them after a disaster.

Make no mistake, a breach by hackers is in fact a disaster and your recovery or continuity policy should follow your incident response plan.

Securing logs

As a pen tester, logs are your source of most of the information you collect and a giant source for information you want to populate in your report. One of the ways hackers conduct APTs is by deleting or updating logs. By swapping, changing, moving, deleting, or altering logs, you have false information or no information about breaches.

Figure 12-9 shows a simple log from Solarwinds called Kiwi that allows me to have a router or switch send their syslog information to a separate server that I can access and review. This way, if a router or other device is rebooted, or a log is deleted or changed, I can get a copy of the log saved off the device itself. Securing logs is a very good recommendation that allows organizations a fighting chance to review and monitor activity on devices that are possibly at risk.

FIGURE 12-9: Saving copies of logs in case a hacker interferes.

Awareness and social engineering

I've said it before, but I have to say it again: The weakest link is the non-technology assets such as your line workers, desktop users, and mobile workforce. They're human, and there's really no way to make 100 percent certain everyone will work diligently to always consider security. This is why awareness training is a must and why it's an ongoing effort.

REMEMBER

The pen test report may show that the network was breached through a social engineering attack that allowed for the login to a centralized system with a user-name and password combo that was provided by a mistaken helpdesk technician. When hackers socially engineer an attack, they can be very believable. Because of this, there needs to be a good mix of technology-based security assets but also a blend of end-user awareness taught through classes, seminars, and webinars to help teach end users about these types of attacks.

>> **Policies:** You'll want to restrict things such as using your personal mobile device for corporate business and your corporate devices for personal business.

>> **Consistent auditing:** This can help to provide feedback on programs and how end users feel about security and their ability to withstand an attack. By pen testing them with a phishing email, you can see whether they click it and give you access. If this happens, you want to see how many end users did this through an audit and use that metric as the basis for getting more training for your workforce.

REMEMBER

People and skills are important to consider. The more your workforce knows about security, the more likely they will suspect an attack and do something about it if they recognize it.

>> **Separation of duties and a need-to-know environment:** Administrators only have access to what they need, not to the entire domain in Windows (as an example). Maybe every network engineer does not need access to the core. Maybe the storage administrator should request higher level access as needed and required.

TIP

By separating these, you can protect your assets with a higher security posture. It also helps to alleviate mistakes.

IN THIS CHAPTER

» **Examining why a retest is a good thing**

» **Testing and retesting . . . and testing and retesting: The reiterative process**

» **Knowing when to retest**

» **Using the report and risk register to choose what to retest**

» **Doing the retest**

Chapter **13**

Retesting

A fter you've conducted a pen test, written your report, and made your recommendations, the next step is to make sure all that work was done correctly for the sake of an increased security posture. What that means is that it's time to retest.

There are important reasons to retest:

» **Ensure the original pen test findings no longer pose a threat.** Or, if they do and you decide to monitor them instead, you can review for any other weaknesses that may be created between the original test and retest.

» **Test the fixes.** This includes what goes into production, the configurations made to fix things, and the services added (or removed). You also want to make sure configuration changes don't expose other issues.

» **Scan any software that was updated.** If software is updated with any patches, security fixes, new drivers, or any other upgrades, it must be vulnerability scanned and retested to ensure it has no exposed points post-remediation.

When you can run a retest and produce a clean and healthy report, this is the final outcome you hope for, but the process is iterative. In this chapter, I cover the fundamentals of conducting a retest and show how the iterative process makes a circular workflow that builds on mitigation and remediation efforts.

Looking at the Benefits of Retesting

After you conclude the phases of pen testing and become more familiar with that process and have made recommendations from the output of your ethical hacking, it's time to do it all over again. This time, however, hopefully when you retest, there is less to find! This is one of many benefits to retesting.

Pen test retesting benefits include:

>> **Testing the ability to respond to incidents.** As you conduct more pen testing efforts, vulnerability scans, mitigation work, and overall security efforts, everyone on the team (and individually) becomes more knowledgeable and better responders. It also builds team cohesion for bigger events.

>> **Testing the ability to harden systems.** Making recommendations and applying them can be a difficult challenge. It's tough to work on systems as it is, but to make radical changes at times and test them, can be tough on the people performing the work. The more this effort takes place, the easier it becomes for people performing it, especially when it comes to paperwork such as change management.

>> **Testing the viability of the risk register.** Your risk register is the central database repository of your critical issues, flaws, and problems. If you're running your pen test program correctly, you have a comprehensive database of all of these issues, but also ways to mitigate them, monitor them, and solution them. Conducting tests and retest value checks your risk register for sure!

>> **Scanning for and finding new issues post remediation.** There is no harm in retesting and getting more scans of your network, penetration testing, and other methods to test security if you're allowed and able to do so! The more you test the more you know and thus, the more secure you will be.

WARNING

Conducting a pen test and then a retest does not mean you are 100 percent secure. Pen testing is a continuous program that doesn't stop. When new systems are deployed, new technology brought online, software is patched or upgraded — to name just a few scenarios — the environment experiences a change that potentially allows a security posture to be weakened. Therefore, you must consider pen testing, reporting, making recommendations, and the retesting phase iterative.

Understanding the Reiterative Nature of Pen Testing and Retesting

Triggers alert you to the need for a retest. Whether you retest (and when) is determined by whoever's in charge, or you may make the suggestion yourself.

Figure 13-1 shows the workflow for both a pen test and a retest, where you find the following workflow items:

1. Start (start the process).

2. Do an assessment of information required to conduct a pen test.

   This may be part of a project plan (or a bigger project program) where you have a stakeholders meeting to gather requirements, as I discuss in Chapter 9. Regardless, when this step is done, you have goals and the scope for your test.

3. Conduct a pen test.

   See Chapter 10 for details.

FIGURE 13-1: The pen testing and retesting processes are very similar.

4. Report out your findings.

Delivering a report, covered in Chapter 11, is likely always a part of your pen testing duties. A subtask or process might be to make recommendations and guide the mitigation process (if that is part of the project scope) and help to work with the risk register.

Technically, at this point, the pen test is complete, but you might be asked to retest.

5. Retest and report on the new findings.

The process could keep going if you don't get the all clear.

6. End of workflow.

Note that the workflows shown in Figure 13-1 are barebones representations of what the process will look like. You might need to include sub processes in additional swim lanes that point to change control/management and other sub process areas.

After you report, make recommendations, and then retest, you absolutely need to re-report it no matter what — even if you don't have any recommendations or items to update on the register. This is why you must continually ask, is the problem solved?

Determining When to Retest

The pen test process flowing into retest (refer to Figure 13-1) should be a trigger-based system where a retest becomes a process task in your pen test program on a continuous basis post your first pen test for the organization. Once that first pen test is done and the workflow begins, retests should be qualified at all times based on the process of reporting, finding remediation, and then retesting.

You can also schedule them on a need basis. In Figure 13-2, I set up a process where the risk register is consulted by priority. If a risk is identified as Tier 1, it's immediately retested as soon as possible. Tier 2 or 3 risks might be able to wait until the monthly or quarterly vulnerability scanning to take place.

REMEMBER

Regardless of how you or your organization sets it up, the truth is, you may not be able to scan whenever you want. This is why change control is so important to follow. You want to know what is on the change calendar and what is going on in the entire organization so there are no conflicts.

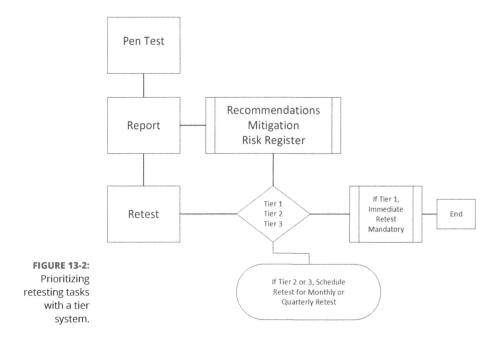

FIGURE 13-2:
Prioritizing
retesting tasks
with a tier
system.

Also, you want to ensure that the retest is followed the same way as the original pen test. The same approvals, process, communication, discussions, and workflow must be followed as was covered in Chapter 10.

Choosing What to Retest

If you've conducted the pen test thoroughly and diligently documented what you did and what you found, deciding what to retest can be, dare I say, easy? You'll rely on your documentation, the report, and the risk register.

Consulting your documentation

In Figure 13-3, I have updated my documentation to reflect what changes were made to the vectors and threats identified in the pen test report. I also took the recommendations provided and some of the risk register items to create a visual of what my report may look like so I can use it as reference when putting together a retest plan.

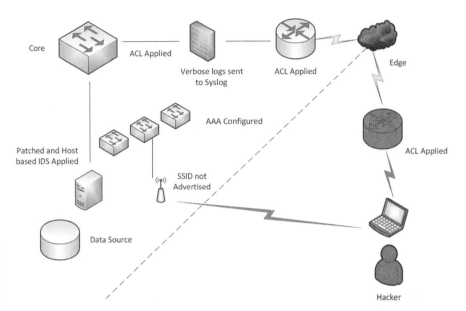

FIGURE 13-3:
My updated
documentation to
reference during
the retest.

Here you can see the suggestions in place and a retest may have blocked all of my vectors to enter the network externally. Some of these examples include:

>> Block the wireless SSID from allowing me to see it and gain access.

>> Use access control lists (ACLs) to block access to critical infrastructure such as routers and switches that stop me from connecting to them.

>> Send logs to a logging facility so that none are wiped away and lost.

>> Patch all systems and use intrusion detection software on critical data systems.

If all this is done, retest all of it to ensure that every one of these changes have in fact worked and more importantly, have not opened other issues or exposed other flaws.

REMEMBER

Running Nessus, Kali, Metasploit, Burp Suite, and Wireshark (amongst others) allow you to identify all these flaws. You should also rerun Nmap to remap the network and search for open ports that may be available. For example, now that you have installed and configured AAA, you may have a new RADIUS server that may need to be patched or secured.

Reviewing the report

The goal of reporting (see Chapter 11) is to focus on what needs to be done based on the goal of the project or the scope of the task you have been given. Defense in depth needs to be considered in all aspects of a retest. You should go back over the original report, documentation, findings, and other items and artifacts and rescan everything you already tested, or you can focus on areas that may have been compromised.

The threat of specific areas should remain the focus, and you should work to mitigate any threats reported in those areas. As I mention in Chapter 11, this is one of the reasons why you don't want to clutter your reports. Some things may be implied such as overall scan of the network. You may want to simply focus on the edge where you were able to gain access via the edge and hop to another router and gain more access.

You'll want to review the report prior to retesting to know where to focus your retesting efforts after mitigations have been implemented. If, for example, a pen test was requested to ensure that the security posture of the web architecture was sound in light of recent concerns made internally by IT professionals, you'll review the report to find:

>> Was the web architecture penetrated?

>> If so, how was this done specifically?

Figure 13-4 shows some of the remediations you may want to make, such as using SSL/TLS, to reduce risks in a web architecture.

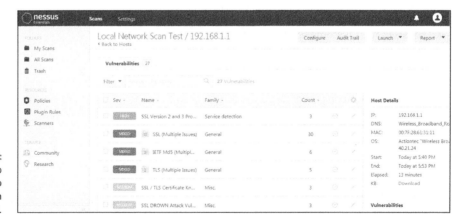

FIGURE 13-4:
Using Nessus to find ways to reduce risks in web architecture.

Reviewing the risk register

By closing an item on the risk register, you can mark it as complete and ready for retest. Consider, as example, two items identified in the pen test report and shown in Table 13-1. Here you can see the item number on the risk register, the priority or tier rating, and the pen tester's notes.

The register could include the recommendations, too, or those can be in a separate document. Whatever the fix is for each item, it needs to be assigned, change control followed to mitigate the issue, and then marked as complete. In this example, the two items found were important to fix to get to the next phase, which is the retest. Depending on the risk and other factors, you can also accept the risk and monitor it if you can't repair it at the time you find it.

A retest will likely show that this issue no longer exists. If a retest flags the issue again, it goes back into the report and the risk register item is reopened.

You must address all risks in a priority manner. As I marked in the notes in Table 13-1, one of the items is a high priority. If the default credentials are not handled immediately, an exploit will likely happen sooner rather than later.

TABLE 13-1   ## Reviewing the Risk Register for Issues to Retest

Pen Test Notes	Tier	Risk Register Entry #
Conducting a pen test on 11/1/xx, an Apache Server Web Server was found running with an IP of 219.3.4.12, which is accessible via port 80 from the public Internet. Having conducted a vulnerability scan and pen test probing the ability to log in, the default credentials were found and able to be used, which allowed full access to the system remotely. This vulnerability requires an immediate response and is labeled Tier 1. Recommendation is to change the default credentials into a honeypot and/or disable access to the default account.	1	17
Conducting a pen test on 11/1/xx, a Cisco Router was found running with an IP of 10.2.11.1, which is accessible via port 23 from the internal corporate network. Having conducted a vulnerability scan and pen test probing the ability to log in, conducting eavesdropping of this device and capturing credentials sent in cleartext, it was found that this device can be accessed and manipulated. This is the default gateway to an access layer network with no access to the distribution or core as it is protected via ACLs. This vulnerability requires a response and is labeled Tier 2. Recommendation is to disable telnet and applied SSH for secure access.	2	24

Running a Pen Retest

To do a pen retest, you follow the same steps from Chapters 9 and 10. You select your tools after your goal and scope have been defined, get appropriate permission and access, set up logging, and then move to gain change control and final approvals to begin. Nothing has changed except you'll focus on specific areas, items, and artifacts derived from the last pen test, the report, and the risk register.

WARNING

Although I point out what you can do as a pen tester earlier in this chapter, you are ethically hacking, so you need to know when and where to stop your attack — you don't want to crash and burn your company or your client's systems.

As you conduct your test, keep these points in mind:

>> **Pay close attention to the old report and what the new information is showing.** For example, you may be re-running Metasploit and finding services, ports, and IPs are responding, some of which may be closed, but others might now be open. For example, in Figure 13-5, you can see that NTP (the network time protocol) service is now operable on a server that wasn't reported with the original pen test scan.

FIGURE 13-5:
Mapping a network and finding new problems.

```
[*] [2019.08.22-09:39:52] Nmap Output: 50501/tcp unknown unknown
[*] [2019.08.22-09:39:52] Nmap Output: 50502/tcp unknown unknown
[*] [2019.08.22-09:39:52] Nmap Output: 50503/tcp unknown unknown
[*] [2019.08.22-09:39:52] Nmap Output: 50504/tcp unknown unknown
[*] [2019.08.22-09:39:52] Nmap Output: 62078/tcp unknown iphone-sync
[*] [2019.08.22-09:39:52] Nmap Output:
[*] [2019.08.22-09:39:52] Nmap Output: OS detection performed. Please report any incorrect results at https://nmap.org/submit/
[*] [2019.08.22-09:39:52] Nmap Output: Nmap done: 254 IP addresses (11 hosts up) scanned in 51.28 seconds
[*] [2019.08.22-09:39:52] Nmap Results: Importing scan data.
[+] [2019.08.22-09:39:56] Workspace:Test Scan Progress:3/177 (1%) Sweeping 192.168.1.1-192.168.1.254 with UDP probes
[*] [2019.08.22-09:39:56] Sending 13 probes to 192.168.1.1->192.168.1.254 (254 hosts)
[*] [2019.08.22-09:39:59] Discovered NTP on 192.168.1.1:123 (24010400000000000000004c4f434ce107de3c00000000c54f234b71b152f3
```

When configurations were made to disable some services, maybe someone accidently turned one on. Or added a new function to secure a service inadvertently turned on a server service you didn't want enabled.

TIP

Whatever the scenario, make note of your exact steps and findings when identifying any new vulnerability. It may be something you pick up on a vulnerability assessment, but for the pen retest, you should try to exploit it.

>> **As you did with the pen test, find a way in.** Using the Nmap ntp-monlist, for example, you can gather information about the NTP server to see what it tells you. Figure 13-6 shows how you can use Nmap to query an NTP server service and identify (or map) it, so you can see what the NTP master server is, the clients, and peers.

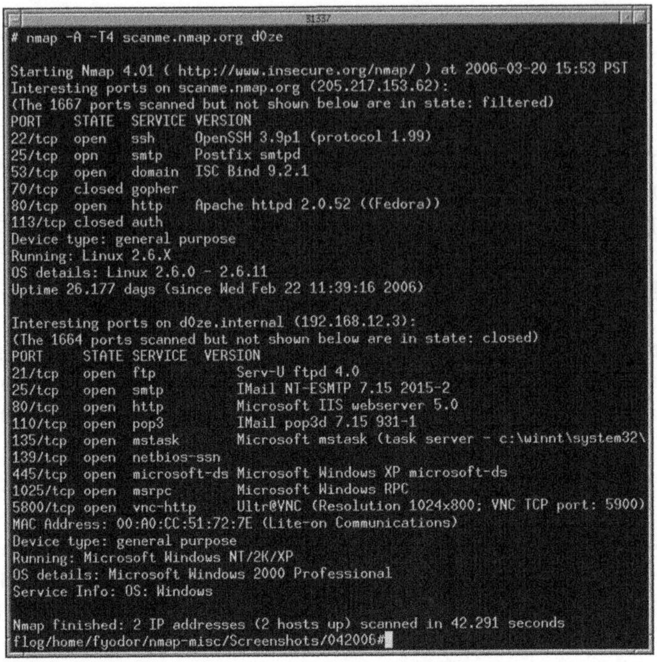

FIGURE 13-6: Using Nmap to exploit NTP.

Through this mapping, you can then attack the master once identified to potentially be crashed with a destroy attack, such as an overflow or DoS, and basically throw the entire network into a tailspin. Document this exploit in your log.

>> **Document your every move.** Just as with the initial pen testing, you must keep detailed notes so that you can write another report with your findings. Most times, you can simply update your first report. However, sometimes you may be asked by your stakeholder to submit a new report entirely that can be reviewed in tandem with the older ones. You will present the new findings to leadership and also have them added to the risk register for remediation by priority or tier level.

5

The Part of Tens

Debunk common pen testing myths.

Improve your pen testing skills with ten tips.

Discover ten resources where you can learn more about pen testing.

Chapter 14

Top Ten Myths About Pen Testing

A *myth* is defined as a phenomenon or a widely held idea or belief that is usually incorrect. When you think about security analysis and doing pen tests, you might have some beliefs that may be wrong. For example, years ago everyone thought that if you were called a hacker you were a bad guy. Now, that's not the case. With white hats, grey hats, and the like, many people these days hear the term hacker and know it isn't always a bad thing.

That said, there are people who believe things like, "Pen testing will secure my organization or provide an adequate amount of security." This is false. Pen testing will *help* to develop your security posture and increase your security level, but it is not the one thing you can rely on to secure your organization completely.

This chapter contains most of the common questions and concerns folks have about what is true and not true about pen testing. Keep these myths in mind, but don't consider them definitive. There's always more to learn.

All Forms of Ethical Hacking Are the Same

Many forms of security analysis take place. As a security professional, knowing which one to conduct at appropriate times is important to understand. Vulnerability assessments, for example, are used to check the status of systems to find and expose weaknesses. Pen testing is the act of actively trying to penetrate security defenses. This includes (and is not limited to) using any tool at your disposal to thwart the security in place to assess whether a vulnerability exists, and if so, whether it can be exploited.

An example would be a tool that checks to see whether you have an open port on a firewall. A pen test (and ethical hacking) is acting in a role to attack and penetrate that port and attempt to gain access, see what you can leverage from there, and continue in hopes of gaining access to valuable data or information.

REMEMBER

Not all forms of ethical hacking are the same. Some are just to find vulnerabilities, other forms are to penetrate the systems, and other forms are to conduct full-scale APTs.

We Can't Afford a Pen Tester

Although many company leaders and department heads believe they need to have security (and also fund it), they might not be aware of the value-add that a real pen tester can bring to their organization nor believe one is worth the cost. So, this myth really has two parts:

>> **Pen testers do not bring value.** A pen tester should be considered the highest level of security analyst you may have employed at your firm. An ethical hacker knows what black hat hackers know. Hackers (and other forms of attackers) is why you have an investment in security in the first place.

A pen tester who can identify and prevent a major breach can save a company not only tangible assets and costs, but also intangible assets and costs such as reputation management. A bank that suffers a breach, for example, will likely lose customer's trust and their business.

>> **Pen testers cost too much.** Whether a company can afford one depends on how much that company is willing to lose in the case of a security incident. My hope is that a book like this can start to bridge the gap because there are ways to lower the costs of pen testing. Maybe train a trusted in-house employee (another IT team member) to use pen testing tools to solve security issues for you.

You're going to pay one way or another. Figure 14-1 shows the volume of data breaches year over year and the volume of records exposed, according to Statista.

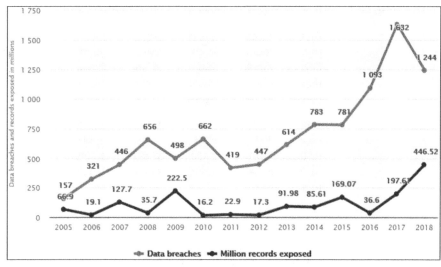

*Source: https://www.statista.com/statistics/273550/
data-breaches-recorded-in-the-united-states-by-number-of-breaches-and-records-exposed/*

The important takeaway from this basic set of metrics is to see that the volume of attempts and penetrations are very, very high and growing. The correlation to the growing amount of records exposed can also be analyzed and quantified various ways, but it's believed that because there is a focus on cybersecurity and penetration testing in the past 10-15 years, the amount of exposure isn't always directly correlated to the volume of attempts.

We Can't Trust a Pen Tester

Some companies are so worried about their sensitive data (secrets, salaries, plans, and so on) that they do not want anyone involved even for the purpose of checking their security. Healthcare organizations especially might be wary because if patient-related information is exposed, that organization is legally liable.

Unfortunately, you can't apply security without giving in to a small amount of vulnerability, but companies need to be smart about it:

» **To do nothing is unwise; to test is smart.** The trick is to find someone who can do the pen testing and who the company trusts. Anyone responsible for hiring a pen tester must explore whether the company has a trusted IT professional in the organization who could be groomed for pen testing.

If that person is you, consider shopping your skills to your organization's leaders to let them know you're interested in that role.

» **An interview process is necessary to reveal the best candidate.** This process should include an extensive background check that looks into financial standings, substance use, and credit standing. If a candidate "passes" these tests, that's good because things like this are clear markers that the person is indeed trustworthy.

» **Audits can help.** An audit process checks the pen tester's work to make sure no wrongdoing took place. This can include spot checking logs, reviewing pen test results, and doing a follow-up with those conducting the tests to validate results. This can help bring peace of mind to those you are vetting or are new to the team.

We Don't Trust the Tools

Beyond building the trust for those conducting a pen test, you must also be comfortable using the toolkit and the tools you build, install, and maintain. This comes in the form of getting reputable tools that are free from malware or are not malware themselves. (Some tools can contain Trojan horse programs that can take over your machine.)

Another concern is that the lack of knowledge in using the tools could create bigger problems by causing a production outage. If a new pen tester (and even a more experienced one) makes a change or uses a tool that somehow has a side effect, it could create more problems than the ones you're trying to identify.

Another concern is about the actual tools themselves being fully operational and free of bugs (problematic software). This is why it's the choice of some elite pen testers to use industry supported tools that are free of bugs or are fixed when found. Because of this, I suggest using vendor supported tools.

Vendor-based tools are the best option for new pen testers to be trusting of their toolkit. Tools such as Wireshark, Nessus, and Nmap are maintained and kept up to date. Figure 14-2 shows how Wireshark is maintained by the vendor. It includes updates, new versions, and bug updates.

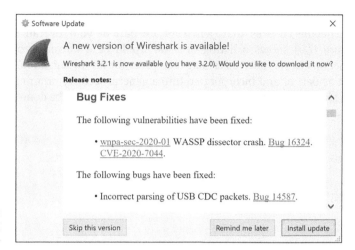

FIGURE 14-2:
Wireshark's bug
fix list.

There are new builds, patches, and a support network built into these tools. I would say that if you download a sketchy application off the Internet to use in your toolkit, properly virus-scanning it prior to using it may help to reduce you infecting yourself or company with a Trojan horse (as an example).

TIP

If you're afraid to use a tool because you're uncertain of its output, then set up tests and test labs and get comfortable with the tools prior to using them. If you know that tools run a ping sweep and you can control the output of it (such as in Nmap), then you may want to start small and build up from there to see in a controlled environment what it will do to your systems. After you start to build up your confidence and trust, you will be more comfortable using the tools.

Pen Tests Are Not Done Often

Pen tests are done all the time. You have to consider the changes in technology, and the dependence on technology that brings more and more of it to the forefront of today's companies. As more devices get connected (think IoT), the more testing will need to take place. The truth is that scanning and testing is a rinse and repeat function. Some big enterprises will create a program in their security operations teams where pen testing is conducted often and usually on a schedule. This is good because the hackers don't operate on a schedule — they are a constant. You should be a constant, too, as well as your pen test program.

A schedule ensures that pen tests are part of your overall security program. Figure 14-3 shows a listing of what would be a normal grouping of security functions, tests, and tasks that take place for an organization. Having your pen test as part of and incorporated into a general security program makes sure that it's always part of the plan of testing. Pen tests can also be done ad hoc as the need arises.

Program Task	Time Period	Scheduled?	Completed?
Change Passwords	3 months	Continuous	Yes
Phishing Tests	6 months	Continuous	Yes
Vulnerability Assessment (Internal Scan)	1 month	Yes	Yes
Vulnerability Assessment (External Scan)	1 month	Yes	Yes
Conduct Penetration Test	3 months	Yes	No
Conduct Incident Response Team Drill	Yearly	No	No
Update Security Documentation (Policies)	Yearly	Yes	No

FIGURE 14-3: A schedule of tests.

REMEMBER

This is similar to the myth that pen tests are good for a period of time. In the spirit of trying to manage an operation, a program or work efforts, leaders may want to believe that by conducting a pen test (and a thorough one at that), they're somehow safe and don't need to conduct a pen test for a period of time. Somehow the reports showed that there is no issues or the issues found have been corrected or being monitored. This is a big misconception. The minute the pen test has been concluded, it is already out of date.

Pen Tests Are Only for Technical Systems

Another constant I always emphasize is the concepts of defense in depth and the need to think outside of the box. Pen tests are very much technical in nature because they're trying to thwart the security of technology assets.

Technology assets can be thwarted and made vulnerable, however, by other than technical means; the two most common being these:

REMEMBER

>> **Physical security:** If a criminal can bypass all firewalls and IDS systems by simply walking into the data center where all the crucial data is hosted and use a thumb drive to snatch data off a server, you've invested a lot of money into something that has been easily bypassed.

What is important about this scenario is that it's common and something you should be considering in your organizations.

It's easy to focus on information technology systems such as computers and infrastructure such as routers, switches, and other networked devices. But you can't forget about physical security; it can also be highly technical. Think of any IoT enabled, network connected and software driven devices. Security cameras, doorbell cameras, and other security devices all fall under your scope, too.

>> **Social engineering:** I don't need to crack your passwords with tools using Kali in my toolkit if I can just call you and trick you into giving them to me. It's easier, quicker, and leaves less of a footprint to be caught with.

Contractors Can't Make Great Pen Testers

A big point of confusion for anyone looking to enhance their security is, do you use in-house resources or outsource to a contractor? Many believe that contractors come from outside of their networks and do not possess the internal knowledge needed to get around their systems and conduct a fair and thorough assessment. This couldn't be farther from the truth.

In-house resources will know the internal network and systems well, but contractors can conduct the same exercises as in-house teams without much difference. If a contractor is given access to the network the same way an in-house resource is, the test will be the same.

The benefit to bringing an outside resource (if even to conduct a yearly pen test) is that they *don't* know your network. If they're able to penetrate it, they have simulated what a hacker would do, which would be to probe, test, map, identify, and attempt to gain access to resources they aren't aware of.

Pen Test Tool Kits Must Be Standardized

In some cases, the standardization of IT assets, systems, programs, tools, and software is a must to remain compliant and have well documented solutions available, but this is not so with pen test tools. The pen tester toolkit will be made by pen testers who use what they need. They may need to keep older tools around for functionality reasons. They may opt to use a different type of packet sniffer because they're more comfortable automating it. There may be cost reasons why some open source software is used instead of costly vendor solutions.

Regardless, whatever you use as a pen tester, you have to manage your own tools and toolkit and the important rule to follow is that you need to make sure you don't wind up a victim yourself. Make sure you take care of your toolkit and keep it safe and updated. If you do that, you don't have to worry about following an IT standard for tools and usage. Your company might mandate something, but as an independent pen tester you should consider using your own tools and what you know works best.

Pen Testing Itself Is a Myth and Unneeded

Hopefully everything you have read in this book has shown you that this is completely untrue. You might find outdated IT processes or workflows that need to be made more efficient or removed completely. You might start to think this way about everything you do and wonder whether pen testing is even needed, doing what you intend it to do, and serving a purpose that provides value.

The return on investment (ROI) of pen testing should be measured to show that the costs associated are warranted. The problem with this thinking is when you're doing a great job keeping all the holes closed because of pen testing. You're keeping the threats in check, and so others might think there is no threat.

REMEMBER

This is why reporting is important in pen testing. To show the actual data points, the metrics and the security applied through reporting, you can show that the investments made are in fact very critical to the security of the information kept on the systems by the company that wants it to be secure.

Pen Testers Know Enough and Don't Need to Continue to Learn

You need to keep learning, developing your skills, and keeping up on the latest technology trends, advancements, and security concerns in the world. You must accept this responsibility and make it a part of your life. You need to keep learning about pen testing, security, and networks, and developing your ethical hacking skillset.

Chapter **15**

Ten Tips to Refine Your Pen Testing Skills

I n this chapter I cover ten tips to help you refine your pen testing skills as you continue in your career or education.

Continue Your Education

Keep learning. Study often and do not limit the scope of your studies. You can get by in your career by learning the basics, getting the tools, and running them. However, you need to learn the finer details of information technology systems, networks, and services and how they are secured or threatened.

The ways you can continue your education are unlimited. However, if on a budget (or have resources to access resources within a budget), here are a few ways you can help yourself:

>> **Use your library.** To access the Internet, books, publications, magazines, and other materials, use your public library system. Some libraries even hold IT classes, and in some cases, even security classes.

>> **Use the Internet.** You can find many sites to help with pen testing, learning about IT, security, and many other topics. (I suggest a few in Chapter 16.) You can gain access to tools and sites that allow you to learn how to conduct penetration testing, and learn operating systems and other valuable programs.

>> **Build a test PC.** If you can gain access to a PC or laptop that you can turn into a test system, acquire it and use it. There are many companies likely have an older system laying around unused that you can turn into a pen test toolkit.

>> **Use virtualization.** Similar to the extra PC or laptop, you can set up virtualization software that allows you access to even more systems so you can build a small virtual network within a computer and you can conduct pen testing on multiple systems from one system. Figure 15-1 shows an example of a tool running within a virtualized system.

>> **Use freeware.** Many demo tools give you full access for a period of time, or at least with limited functionality, that you can use to learn with.

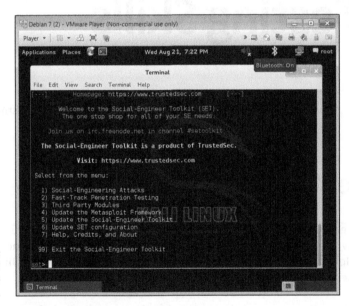

FIGURE 15-1: Using Kali and VMware virtualization.

Build Your Toolkit

Carpenters and other trades rely on their tools to be able to do their jobs. Auto mechanics, welders, and others who use tools to conduct their work can't do great work without tools that are maintained and preserved. The same is true of IT professionals, especially those who function in the security realm as pen testers.

No matter what, consider your tools as the most important thing you can maintain. Keep the following in mind as you build your toolkit:

>> **Keeping your toolkit current is one of the hardest things to do as a pen tester.** You will find some tools (sometimes older tools) are more helpful to getting the results you need. Some tools are scripts that are created and maintained by each individual pen tester.

>> **Some tools are expensive, and you need to license for them.** You also need to keep them updated. For example, any tools, software, programs, applications, and systems you use need to be patched, virus scanned, updated, and kept up to date.

>> **All software must be updated.** Any software that requires signature files, digital certificates, block ciphers, and any other form of additional software needs to be updated and maintained.

>> **Technology changes over time.** There will be updates to the systems you use, and there will be different systems in different organizations — all this means you need to keep your toolkit current with new additions as you find you need them.

>> **Make sure your computer is updated and safe.** Make sure you keep the system you run all this on current as well. Nothing is worse than the embarrassment of getting your own system hacked as a pen tester. Keep your own stuff pristine, secure, and tested.

Think outside the Box

Never get comfortable with the same vectors, tools, patterns, and attacks. Always consider another option. The plan B. You have to constantly think outside the box to stay ahead of those who commit crimes. Think of hackers and attacks like running water. It will find a way. You too need to think like running water and consider, anticipate, and get ahead of different types of attacks and vectors for attacks by developing this dynamic mindset.

I talk a lot about vectors in this book. In Figure 15-2, I show an example of a planned penetration test where I want to enter the network via the wireless access point. In a situation where I am working with an organization that has given me the ability to try another path if possible, I have found another way through the Internet connection (plan B) to access the network externally. I could also have accessed the network from picking up a signal from the parking lot.

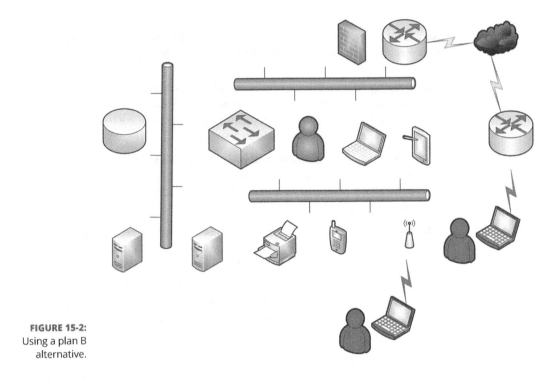

Think Like a Hacker

You need to know what hackers do. As an ethical person, it's not easy to think like a criminal. This is where the great pen testers excel. You have to think beyond what a good guy would do . . . what someone who has ethics would do.

Ways to help you develop this is by reading. You can read attacks that took place in the past to learn about those who conducted them. One of the oldest hackers of the past is Kevin Mitnick who conducted hacks back in the '90s when he was arrested in 1995. Learning about Kevin and how he turned into a grey hat hacker over time helps to get inside the mind of those who conduct crimes and their motives.

Get Involved

Whether it be conferences, online communities, or social outlets online or in per-son, spend some time networking with others in your field.

Two conferences where you can continue your education, learn specifics of pen testing from experts in the field, meet book authors, and get access to current trends and classes about current products is Defcon (www.defcon.org) and Blackhat (www.blackhat.com). Normally both are held in the United States, but over the years the conference has grown and expanded to other countries as well. Both of these sites will have options to sign up for a conference, but have other options as well to view older media, papers and research conducted over the years. It is also a great way to meet other experts in your field as you continue to grow within it.

There are professional organizations that cater to pen testers, schools that form groups of likeminded individuals, governance committees, and other types of groups that allow those who conduct ethical hacking to join together and share ideas. There are government agencies that you can join to work more closely with LEO and military or other government agencies to share ideas and information.

Chapter 16 offers some websites where you can investigate options; however, a simple Google search can provide you with a wealth of ideas and information.

TIP

Regardless of who you join up with, a community-based approach to sharing ideas has led to some of the larger crowdsharing/crowdsourcing and other group-like successes there are today. Pair up and work on some projects together to share ideas and learn more about pen testing.

Use a Lab

If you buy and build one, rent space, or lease system time from others, use online resources available to you for testing or through the use of virtual machines in a lab you build — hands-on time is crucial to your success. You need to be able to run the tools, hacks, tests, and see what is possible. It's one of the best ways to learn how to become an elite pen tester.

Because there are many challenges to do this, you can still learn ways to get hands-on training:

>> **Online test sites:** I provide links in Chapter 16.

>> **A test machine:** You can also set up on one computer in your home a virtual system of other machines (a virtual network) and test the systems on your base machine.

Figure 15-3 lays out a nice lab strategy you can use to start to develop a pen testing practice lab at work or at home.

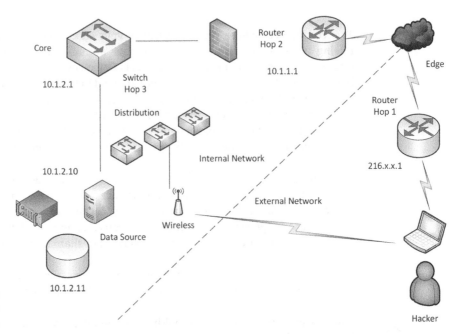

FIGURE 15-3:
Creating a
viable lab.

Some of the items you may want to consider in building your lab may include (but not limited to):

>> **Server infrastructure:** You can either set up a server physically on your mock network or a virtual one. Either way, make sure that you have allocated resources so that you can configure targets such as a database (can be large in size), as well as multiple network connections for redundancy (cluster) or other advanced setups.

>> **Network infrastructure:** From the cabling to the wireless systems — the routers, switches, access points, firewalls, and everything in between — you can configure all the network components to interconnect the devices you want to set up as resources on your mock network.

>> **Pen test system:** The point of origin, which can be the laptop that you use as an ethical hacker to conduct the penetration testing.

As you learn more and more, you can add systems and infrastructure to further build out the lab so you can conduct more tests.

Stay Informed

Just like any other role, skill, or function, the more you know the better off you will be. Up-to-date threat information can help you learn about the myriad of attacks and patterns coming out daily. This information deepens your knowledge of what you need to be aware of as a pen tester protecting against them.

REMEMBER

You should also stay abreast of things going on in the pen test community. One great way to do this is by meeting up with others in your field (as I advise in the "Get Involved," section earlier in this chapter).

Stay Ahead of New Technologies

Technology is always changing. Remember when virtualization became important? Cloud? Wireless? Mobile? As each of these technologies emerged (and in some instances converged), it was important to stay on top of them because the minute they came to market, there seemed to be a ton of attacks that came right along with them. When wireless hit the market, for example, there were drive-by scanners hanging out of cars — hackers were cracking into systems in companies from the parking lot. You must know about new technologies, learning about them, and anticipating how black hat hackers might use them.

There are countless resources available to learn of new technology. For example, if you know your primary targets are going to be Cisco, Citrix, Microsoft, VMWare, Linux (select a distribution), and EMC Storage, you may want to add yourself to those vendors' websites and their mailing lists to stay ahead of updates, new patches, version updates, and so on. If you have a contract with any of these vendors, they should be sending you information; however, anyone can contact these vendors and be added to their mailing lists so you can learn more about them. For example, if you were a large Cisco networking customer, you can gain access to RSS feeds, field notices, security advisories, bug alerts, software updates, and so much more.

Build Your Reputation

Building your reputation is easy. For someone (anyone) to let you into these protected networks where all their data sits, they absolutely must trust you. Trust. It's the critical piece of the proverbial pie of your career in pen testing. Identify as someone who can't be trusted, and it's likely you will never work for a company that needs your assistance in thwarting crime again.

This means you cannot be a criminal! You need to make sure you act professionally and ethically. Build your network of peers and people who can vouch for you and continue to act in a way that is honorable and as a consummate professional.

Learn about Physical Security

All the technical knowledge, skill, tools, and experience in the world can't save you and a company from a social engineering attack. Nothing can thwart technical security faster than social engineering. Card swipes, magnetic door locks, bio-sensor reading, cameras, physical security guards, wall hopping, and all of the other things that fall outside of the computer network where data is kept can't stop someone from breaking and entering. Always consider physical security challenges as a pen tester and augment your technical vulnerability analysis and scans with checking how physical security and defense in depth stacks up.

Chapter **16**

Ten Sites to Learn More About Pen Testing

As an IT professional, it doesn't matter how much you know today — there is always more to learn! I can assure you that what you know today could become outdated as technology evolves and morphs into new innovations. With that said, in this chapter I point you to ten sites online that I know will be extremely helpful to you not only as a pen tester but as a security professional in general.

WARNING

If any of the websites are no longer assessible at any time, do your own online searches for keywords such as pen testing, penetration testing, and security hacking. Also make sure to fact check any data not coming from a reputable site. The sites I list here are generally reputable, but you should still consider researching things before you implement them regardless.

TIP

One of the best sources of information you can use for your studies is in the help files of your software. If you use the knowledge bases that come with the tool and online at the vendor's website, you will learn how to better use the tools and help to reinforce some of the topics you learned in this book.

SANS Institute

```
https://www.sans.org
```

SANS.org leads to the SANS Institute where since 1989 the site has been filled with a large amount of useful security information that is freely accessible to all. This online resource is easily searchable from the home page and within it contains many resources a pen tester can use, including the SANS Information Security Reading Room that hosts approximately 3,000 original research papers in 110 important categories of security.

You can sign up for weekly bulletins, alerts, newsletters, risk alerts, and other email items that can keep you abreast of threats. You can also access the Internet Storm Center, which is an early warning system for threats.

There are many other resources available such as templates, vendor product information, information on open and closed source software, and so much more.

Another point of interest on the SANS website as shown in Figure 16-1 is the connection to their focused areas on pen testing at

```
https://pen-testing.sans.org/
```

TIP

If you're looking to make pen testing a career, being connected to this community and digging deep into their online resources can help made a value add to your education and knowledge.

FIGURE 16-1:
SANS.org.

GIAC Certifications

```
https://www.giac.org
```

Another point of interest on the SANS website is the connection to their certification arm of SANS, which is called GIAC (Global Information Assurance Certification). GIAC is focused on different areas of security, such as incident response and handling, forensic, and of course pen testing. You can get directly to their GPEN certification (see Figure 16-2) at

```
https://www.giac.org/certifications/pen-testing
```

Aside from being an industry standard exam that tests your ability to conduct a pen test, the GIAC.org site also has a wealth of information about pen testing. You'll need to pay for the exam and the study materials that come with it. There are other tests available such as CompTIA's Pentest+ and others, but the benefit to getting GPEN certified is that you get to connect to a community of expert pen testers as well as getting certified and educated.

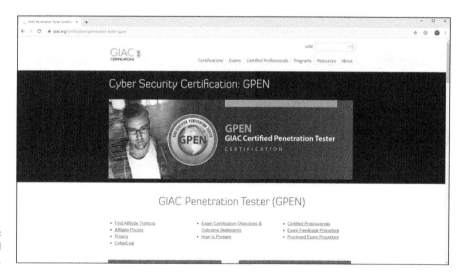

FIGURE 16-2:
The GIAC GPEN
certification.

Software Engineering Institute

```
sei.cmu.edu
```

Carnegie Mellon University (CMU) has long been a source of amazing security information. You'll find information about risk assessments, pen testing, forensics, and security-based incident handling. The CMU site has a CERT landing page that hosts publications and other scholarly works about cybersecurity:

```
https://www.sei.cmu.edu/about/divisions/cert/
```

CERT partners with industry experts (from areas such as technology industry, law, government, and academia) to provide advanced studies and research on relevant topics.

(Assorted) Legal Penetration Sites

Legal penetration sites are variously hosted by groups that provide a realistic way for ethical hackers to learn real hacking skills on networks and systems that have been left in a semi-hardened state. If you run a search on Google for "Legal Penetration Sites," you will pull up reputable sources to find these sites.

Cisco.com has information in their help forums as well as security magazines (another great resource) and other sites that host these penetration test hubs where you can hone your skills.

TIP

If you can't afford to set up your own lab environment for testing purposes, then seeking outside resources such as this can really help develop your skills.

Open Web Application Security Project

```
https://www.owasp.org/
```

The Open Web Application Security Project (OWASP) was established in 2001 and is currently a not-for-profit organization that works on the foundation of group collaboration. OWASP is a group that boasts open source and does so with no affiliation of any kind. Their focus is on web application hacking and the security of applications, software, web apps, and programs.

The frameworks, information, and resources provided help to guide a pen tester into areas of risk and vulnerabilities surrounding applications such as hacking APIs.

```
https://www.owasp.org/index.php/Category:Vulnerability
```

This site can really help you better understand more in-depth details about SQL injection, fuzzing, and other topics surrounding programing and software hacking, and what you should seek to penetrate and exploit these systems as an ethical hacker. Figure 16-3 shows the top ten application security risks at the any time.

FIGURE 16-3: The top ten application risks on the Open Web Application Security Project.

Tenable

```
https://www.tenable.com
```

Tenable makes Nessus, and you can visit the website for more information on vulnerability scanning, pen testing, and risk assessments. One of the greatest things you can find on the Tenable website is a series of tools and information primarily focused on pen testing. In their research papers are details on how to become a better pen tester:

```
https://www.tenable.com/research
```

Figure 16-4 shows the Tenable website where you can download Nessus for trial use, or purchase a license for permanent use.

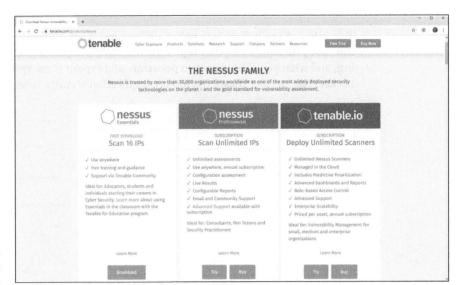

Nmap

```
https://nmap.org/
```

Nmap is undeniably one of the hottest and most used tools for pen testing outside of Nessus and Metasploit. Contained in Kali, Nmap is a tool that can really do it all. On the website you will find advanced usage of the tool to include subverting firewalls, spoofing scans, getting around IDS, automation and scripting of the tool, and so much more.

Wireshark

```
https://www.wireshark.org
```

Wireshark is one of the de facto tools in your toolkit and a primary source of information for troubleshooting networks, information gathering, or pen testing.

```
https://www.wireshark.org/#learnWS
```

Within the main website you will find tons of detailed information on how to use this tool. As well, the forums where engineers talk about issues and things they find are loaded with literally thousands of pieces of valuable information that will help you learn more about networking, TCP/IP, the Internet, and how packets and frames traverse a network.

TIP

Need to learn more about ports, channels, communication, sockets, protocols, packets, headers, and so on? This is the site you need to go to learn more about these details.

Dark Reading

```
https://www.darkreading.com
```

In today's pen testing world, one of the go-to sites for security professionals is Dark Reading. Dark Reading helps provide information not only on old but breaking news stories geared towards an online community of security gurus and professionals looking for more information about topics like pen testing.

You'll find newsletters and feeds and the sections on Attacks and Breaches can help you emulate scenarios in your pen testing, stay on top of trends, and conduct ethical hacks to test your security posture.

Offensive Security

```
https://www.offensive-security.com/
```

From the distributors of Kali, Offensive Security is a company that specializes in doing penetration testing. Offensive Security offers penetration testing services as a service, and they provide a certification as well. On this site, shown in Figure 16-5, you can learn more about pen testing from the experts who do it day in and day out. You'll find sample checklists, tools, reports, and a lot of the things you might want to emulate in your own pen tests.

FIGURE 16-5:
Gain access
to Kali.

Index

hacktivists, 36

handshakes, TCP/IP, 107

hardening. *See also* recommendations
  network, 165–166
  role in prevention, 142–143
  systems, 168–173

health industry, security scenarios in, 24

Health Insurance Portability and
  Accountability Act (HIPAA) of 1996, 35

heuristical scanning, 33–34

high-level risks, in risk register, 158

holistic approach to security practices, 11

honeypots, 164, 169, 178

hop by hop strategy, 130, 165, 167

hosts
  looking at with Wireshark, 45, 46
  Nessus scans identifying vulnerable, 95
  ping sweeps, 31–32
  sending flood attacks to, 83–84
  simulating subvert attacks against, 105–108
  vulnerability scanning, 21

I

ICMP (Internet Control Message Protocol),
  31–32, 90

icons, explained, 2

identification of risks, as goal of pen testing,
  24–26

IDS (intrusion detection software), 33

impact of pen testing, dealing with, 127

incident response (incident handling)
  as goal of pen testing, 29–30
  testing with pen retest, 182

incorrect information, excluding from
  reports, 157

infiltration
  in APTs, 114
  assessment of, 140
  in internal pen testing, 136
  in pen testing, 130, 131–133

Information Gathering menu (Kali), 104, 105

infrastructure
  in lab, 206
  recommendations for, 171–172

in-house security pros, 9–10, 199

inside threats, 82

intense scans, with Nmap, 105–106

internal attacks
  conducting, 136
  in testing strategy, 20

internal networks
  network segmentation, 166–167
  overwhelm and disrupt attacks, 82
  recommendations for, 167
  testing, 61

Internet, continuing education through, 202

Internet Control Message Protocol (ICMP),
  31–32, 90

Internet of Things (IoT), 12, 54

Internet protocol (IP), 12, 13

Internet protocol (IP) addresses
  in infiltration stage of pen testing, 132–133
  IP address spoofing attacks, 74–75

Internet Protocol Security (IPsec), 65

interviewing pen testers, 196

intrusion detection software (IDS), 33

intrusion prevention software (IPS), 33

Inundator tool (Kali), 81

IP fragmentation attacks, 88–89

iterative process, pen testing as, 183–184

J

jump drives, assumption attacks through, 78

K

Kali Linux toolset
  fragmentation attack tools, 88–89
  overview, 46–49
  overwhelm and disrupt attacks, 80–82

N

P

packets
  buffer overflow attacks, 87
  eavesdropping, 75–76
  fragmentation attacks, 88–89
  packet capture, 13, 14, 77
  smurf attacks, 90
  tiny packet attacks, 91
  Xmas tree attacks, 91–92
passive reconnaissance, 38
password capture hacks, 45
password cracking, 62–63, 133, 134
passwords
  looking at with Wireshark, 45
  in network hardening, 165
  preventing social engineering attacks, 59
  recommendations for, 178
  vulnerabilities related to, 27, 29
past test results, reviewing, 122, 123
patching
  patch audits, 94–95
  patch schedule, 174
  program for, 169
  systems, 32–33
Payment Card Industry Data Security
    Standard (PCI DSS), 35
penetration and exploitation attacks
  cryptology and encryption, 63–65
  Metasploit Pro tool, 65–67
  overview, 53–54
  types of
    client-side and server-side attacks, 60–62
    overview, 55
    password cracking, 62–63
    social engineering, 55–60
  vectors and hacking, understanding, 54–55
penetration step, in pen testing, 130, 133–
    134, 140–141

penetration testing (pen testing). *See also*
    recommendations; reporting; *specific
    attack types*
  affordability of, 194–195
  assessment
    exfiltration, 141–142
    exploitation, 141
    infiltration, 140
    overview, 139
    penetration, 140–141
  certification, 10
  conducting tests
    APT, 131, 135
    attack steps, 130–136
    documentation, 136–139
    exfiltration, 131, 135
    exploitation, 131, 134
    infiltration, 130, 131–133
    from inside, 136
    next steps after attack, 135–136
    other capture methods and vectors, 139
    overview, 129–130
    penetration, 130, 133–134
  cybercrime considerations, 16–18
  frequency of, 197–198
  general steps in, 21–22
  goals of
    asset protection, 24
    finding vulnerabilities, 26–27
    incident response, 29–30
    overview, 23–24
    risk identification, 24–26
    scanning and assessing, 27–28
    securing operations, 28
  holistic approach to security practices, 11
  myths about, 193–200
  need for, 200
  overview, 1–3, 7–8

risk register *(continued)*
  overview, 25–26
  testing viability of, 182
  updating, 138, 158–159
roles
  in incident response, 30
  of involved parties, clarifying, 118, 119
router hopping, 61, 165, 167
routers
  buffer overflow attacks, 86–87
  identifying DoS attacks on, 85
  subvert attacks against, 105–106, 109–110

S

safe environment, pen testing in, 19, 21
sales industry, security scenarios in, 24
sandbox (lab)
  building, 205–206
  pen testing in, 19
SANS Institute, 210
scan maintenance
  antivirus and other technologies, 33–34
  compliance, 34–35
  exclusions and ping sweeps, 31–32
  patching, 32–33
scan type, selecting, 125
scanning. *See also* vulnerability scanning
  for destroy attacks, 94–97
  as goal of pen testing, 27–28
  heuristical, 33–34
  with Metasploit Pro, 65
  Nessus tool for, 40–42
  for new issues after remediation, 182
  with Nmap, 105–108
  Wireshark tool for, 43–46
scheduling pen testing, 19
scope, pen testing, 119–120, 151, 155

screen scraping, 38
script kiddies, 36
Secure Shell (SSH), 64
Secure Sockets Layer (SSL), 64
security. *See also* penetration testing;
    recommendations; *specific attacks*
  defense in depth, 11, 29, 149
  general recommendations, 173–177
  as goal of pen testing, 28
  incident response, 29–30
  network, in prevention of spoofing, 75
  of pen test reports, 158
  physical, 97, 102, 198–199, 208
  role of pen testing in
    certification, 10
    cybercrime considerations, 16–18
    general steps in testing, 21–22
    holistic approach to security practices, 11
    overview, 1–3, 7–8
    pen tester roles, 8–10
    preparing for testing, 18–19
    skills needed, 10–16
    strategy for testing, 19–21
  toolkit, 40
security analysts, 9–10
security consultants, 10
security incident handlers, 17
security posture, assessing, 19–21
segmentation, network
  recommendations for, 166–167
  and virtualization, 177
SEP (Symantec Endpoint Protection),
    112, 113
separation of duties, 180
servers
  in lab, 206
  recommendations for, 169–170
server-side attacks, 60–62

wired networks, recommendations for, 168

wireless networks

  inside, as attack vector, 61

  in internal pen testing, 136

  recommendations for, 168

Wireshark tool

  for assumption attacks, 72–74

  eavesdropping, 75–76

  overview, 43–46

  packet capture and analysis, 77

  tiny packet attacks, identifying, 91

  tuning with filters, 125–126

  vendor support for, 196–197

Wireshark website, 214–215

worms, 98

X

xhydra tool (Kali), 133, 134

Xmas tree attacks, 91–92

Z

Zenmap, 49–50

zero days, 98

zombies, 75, 80, 84–85

About the Author

Rob Shimonski (www.shimonski.com) is an experienced entrepreneur and an active participant in the business community. Rob is a bestselling author and editor with over 25 years' experience developing, producing, and distributing print media in the form of books, magazines, and periodicals. To date, Rob has successfully contributed to over 100 books that are currently in circulation. Rob has written over 25 of those books specializing on security covering intricate topics such as penetration testing, incident handling, cyberwarfare, and the deployment of advanced network and security tools and technologies. Rob has worked for many large-scale global companies including the US Military, Microsoft, Cisco, the National Security Agency (NSA), and Northwell Health. Rob also served as a veteran of the United States Marine Corps.

As a leader, technologist, security practitioner, penetration tester, incident responder/handler and network architect, Rob has led numerous efforts to architect, design, strategize, and implement enterprise solutions that must be and remain secure. Working for government, military, health, and technology entities has shown Rob not only the importance of responding to protecting assets, testing for and finding issues as well as handling critical incidents, but what is at risk. Rob has spent over two decades taking what he has learned in real-world scenarios and teach others through his published books, videos, and articles.

Rob is also a well-known expert in the analysis of protocols with tools such as Wireshark and has written multiple books on protocol analysis, capture, and decoding. As a technology, crisis, and security expert, Rob has helped companies find weaknesses and how to secure them correctly, respond to incidents, and be proactive in monitoring for them as well as preventing and stopping them.

One of the more interesting contracts Rob has taken as a penetration tester (and able to disclose) is when he was featured in Men's Health Magazine having been hired by the parent company to infiltrate and exfiltrate the corporate network and remain undetected (https://www.menshealth.com/technology-gear/a19528048/protect-yourself-online/).

Dedication

This book is dedicated to Dylan and Vienna. Watching you grow and being a part of your life has forever defined mine. I love being your Dad. Love always and forever.

Acknowledgements

Writing a book is a team sport. Unless you have embarked on a project of this magnitude, it's hard to put into words how 8-10 months fly by and how many people are involved in that year to make a book even better than you imagined it. Having been officially writing books since 1998 (my first), I cannot believe it's now 2020 and to look back at all of the connections I have made, the friends, family, and partnerships. . . it's truly amazing.

I can't thank the team who helped me put *Penetration Testing For Dummies* together enough for their belief, support, guidance, and efforts throughout the process.

Nicole, Rebecca, Katie, Ashley, and Teddy — thank you for helping me make a better book. I am grateful. The team assembled to write a Dummies book is by far some of the best in the business! Thank you for the opportunity to shine.

I also want to thank all those who have mentored me, worked with me, spent time either leading me or being led by me. It truly is gratifying to have come across the paths of so many great people in my time in business and IT. An extra special thank you to those at Northwell who have believed in my abilities and to all those who I have had the honor and privilege to work with.

Lastly (and most importantly), thank you to my family. Without you, I would not have the support needed to write a book in my free time (if there is such a thing) and be supportive and motivating me when things conflicted and time was tough to come by. I appreciate you all more than you will ever know.

Publisher's Acknowledgments

Executive Editor: Lindsay Lefevere

Development Editor: Rebecca Senninger

Technical Editor: Teddy Guzek

Production Editor: Mohammed Zafar Ali

Cover Image: © bygermina/Shutterstock

Take dummies with you everywhere you go!

Whether you are excited about e-books, want more from the web, must have your mobile apps, or are swept up in social media, dummies makes everything easier.

Find us online!

dummies.com

Leverage the power

Dummies is the global leader in the reference category and one of the most trusted and highly regarded brands in the world. No longer just focused on books, customers now have access to the dummies content they need in the format they want. Together we'll craft a solution that engages your customers, stands out from the competition, and helps you meet your goals.

Advertising & Sponsorships

Connect with an engaged audience on a powerful multimedia site, and position your message alongside expert how-to content. Dummies.com is a one-stop shop for free, online information and know-how curated by a team of experts.

- Targeted ads
- Video
- Email Marketing
- Microsites
- Sweepstakes sponsorship

20 MILLION PAGE VIEWS EVERY SINGLE MONTH

15 MILLION UNIQUE VISITORS PER MONTH

43% OF ALL VISITORS ACCESS THE SITE VIA THEIR MOBILE DEVICES

700,000 NEWSLETTER SUBSCRIPTIONS TO THE INBOXES OF

300,000 UNIQUE INDIVIDUALS EVERY WEEK

# of dummies

Custom Publishing

Reach a global audience in any language by creating a solution that will differentiate you from competitors, amplify your message, and encourage customers to make a buying decision.

- Apps
- Books
- eBooks
- Video
- Audio
- Webinars

Brand Licensing & Content

Leverage the strength of the world's most popular reference brand to reach new audiences and channels of distribution.

For more information, visit dummies.com/biz

PERSONAL ENRICHMENT

Staying Sharp
9781119187790
USA $26.00
CAN $31.99
UK £19.99

Facebook
9781119179030
USA $21.99
CAN $25.99
UK £16.99

Guitar
9781119293354
USA $24.99
CAN $29.99
UK £17.99

Investing
9781119293347
USA $22.99
CAN $27.99
UK £16.99

Beekeeping
9781119310068
USA $22.99
CAN $27.99
UK £16.99

Digital Photography
9781119235606
USA $24.99
CAN $29.99
UK £17.99

Meditation
9781119251163
USA $24.99
CAN $29.99
UK £17.99

Pregnancy
9781119235491
USA $26.99
CAN $31.99
UK £19.99

Samsung Galaxy S7
9781119279952
USA $24.99
CAN $29.99
UK £17.99

iPhone
9781119283133
USA $24.99
CAN $29.99
UK £17.99

Crocheting
9781119287117
USA $24.99
CAN $29.99
UK £16.99

Nutrition
9781119130246
USA $22.99
CAN $27.99
UK £16.99

PROFESSIONAL DEVELOPMENT

Windows 10
9781119311041
USA $24.99
CAN $29.99
UK £17.99

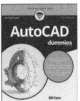
AutoCAD
9781119255796
USA $39.99
CAN $47.99
UK £27.99

Excel 2016
9781119293439
USA $26.99
CAN $31.99
UK £19.99

QuickBooks 2017
9781119281467
USA $26.99
CAN $31.99
UK £19.99

macOS Sierra
9781119280651
USA $29.99
CAN $35.99
UK £21.99

LinkedIn
9781119251132
USA $24.99
CAN $29.99
UK £17.99

Windows 10 All-in-One
9781119310563
USA $34.00
CAN $41.99
UK £24.99

SharePoint 2016
9781119181705
USA $29.99
CAN $35.99
UK £21.99

Fundamental Analysis
9781119263593
USA $26.99
CAN $31.99
UK £19.99

Networking
9781119257769
USA $29.99
CAN $35.99
UK £21.99

Office 2016
9781119293477
USA $26.99
CAN $31.99
UK £19.99

Office 365
9781119265313
USA $24.99
CAN $29.99
UK £17.99

Salesforce.com
9781119239314
USA $29.99
CAN $35.99
UK £21.99

Coding
9781119293323
USA $29.99
CAN $35.99
UK £21.99

dummies.com

dummies
A Wiley Brand

Learning Made Easy

ACADEMIC

9781119293576
USA $19.99
CAN $23.99
UK £15.99

9781119293637
USA $19.99
CAN $23.99
UK £15.99

9781119293491
USA $19.99
CAN $23.99
UK £15.99

9781119293460
USA $19.99
CAN $23.99
UK £15.99

9781119293590
USA $19.99
CAN $23.99
UK £15.99

9781119215844
USA $26.99
CAN $31.99
UK £19.99

9781119293378
USA $22.99
CAN $27.99
UK £16.99

9781119293521
USA $19.99
CAN $23.99
UK £15.99

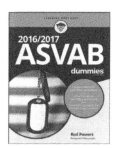

9781119239178
USA $18.99
CAN $22.99
UK £14.99

9781119263883
USA $26.99
CAN $31.99
UK £19.99

Available Everywhere Books Are Sold

Small books for big imaginations

9781119177173
USA $9.99
CAN $9.99
UK £8.99

9781119177272
USA $9.99
CAN $9.99
UK £8.99

9781119177241
USA $9.99
CAN $9.99
UK £8.99

9781119177210
USA $9.99
CAN $9.99
UK £8.99

9781119262657
USA $9.99
CAN $9.99
UK £6.99

9781119291336
USA $9.99
CAN $9.99
UK £6.99

9781119233527
USA $9.99
CAN $9.99
UK £6.99

9781119291220
USA $9.99
CAN $9.99
UK £6.99

9781119177302
USA $9.99
CAN $9.99
UK £8.99

Unleash Their Creativity

dummies.com

Printed and bound by CPI Group (UK) Ltd, Croydon, CR0 4YY

09/06/2025